Addiction Recovery

A movement for social change and personal growth in the UK

David Best

Pavilion

Professional

Addiction Recovery: A movement for social change and personal growth in the UK

Published by:
Pavilion Publishing (Brighton) Ltd
Richmond House
Richmond Road
Brighton
BN2 3RL
Tel: 01273 623222
Fax: 01273 625526
Email: info@pavpub.com

Published 2012

Pavilion Professional is an imprint of Pavilion Publishing, which aims to address the issues important to higher level professionals and academics.

A catalogue record for this book is available from the British Library.

ISBN: 978-1-908066-16-9

Pavilion is the leading training and development provider and publisher in the health, social care and allied fields, providing a range of innovative training solutions underpinned by sound research and professional values. We aim to put our customers first, through excellent customer service and value.

Author: David Best
Production editor: Catherine Ansell-Jones, Pavilion
Cover design: Emma Garbutt, Pavilion
Page layout and typesetting: Katherine Paine, Pavilion
Printing: Charlesworth Press

Contents

Foreword

William L White, author of *Pathways from the Culture of Addiction to the Culture of Recovery* and *Slaying the Dragon: The history of addiction treatment and recovery in America*

An emerging international addiction recovery advocacy movement is positing recovery as a new organising paradigm for alcohol and drug-related social policies and is transforming traditional addiction treatment from a focus on acute bio-psycho-social stabilisation or palliative care to a focus on sustained recovery management. There are unique variations in this movement as it traverses national and cultural borders – different inciting forces, sources of resistance, core ideas, goals, strategies and degrees of early achievements. Dr David Best has provided a significant contribution in this first academic but highly readable text on the recovery advocacy movement in the UK.

This handbook is an essential primer for those wanting to understand how the recovery advocacy movement is impacting addiction-related policy, research, treatment and grassroots recovery support in the UK. Best takes us through a journey of exploration spanning the meaning of recovery and recovery capital, recovery rates, the distinction between recovery and treatment, and the importance of peer support in the long-term recovery process. He then takes us on a sweeping tour of the recovery advocacy movement within specific local communities in the UK and how the larger movement is influencing government policies in England and Scotland.

This heightened focus on recovery marks a shift from a focus on the problem or the latest clinical intervention to a focus on the lived solution and the role of indigenous community support in long-term recovery. The resulting vision is one of enhancing resilience and resistance to addiction, engaging people at earlier stages of problem development, facilitating the transition from recovery initiation to recovery maintenance, enhancing the quality of personal and family life in long-term recovery, and breaking the intergenerational transmission of alcohol and other drug problems. The assertive pursuit of that vision is producing profound changes in long-standing ideas, policies and programmes. This handbook provides a compelling roadmap of this new world. In this new world, people who were once part of the problem are now being mobilised to become part of the solution. When a definitive history of the movement is finally written in the decades to come, Best's book will be an invaluable resource.

Chapter 1

The origins of the recovery movement

What does 'recovery' mean?

Words get in the way of defining recovery. In one sense it seems self-evident that the aim of treatment is to generate recovery, but recovery has come to mean something entirely different from this lay definition. Recovery has come to be a kind of social movement; one that has exercised clinicians, commissioners and policymakers in the UK and has received relatively little discussion or consideration from academics. It has come to mean something different from both what has been done previously and from 'treatment', and it is difficult to capture.

The addictions field is not short of definitions with two of the most widely cited derived from 'expert' groups – one in the UK and the other in the US.

'Voluntarily sustained control over substance use which maximises health and well-being and participation in the rights, roles and responsibilities of society.' (UK Drug Policy Commission, 2008, p6)

'A voluntarily maintained lifestyle characterised by sobriety, personal health and citizenship.' (Betty Ford Institute Consensus Panel, 2007, p222)

In a similar vein, the Scottish Government's *The Road to Recovery* defined recovery as *'a process through which an individual is enabled to move from their problem drug use, towards a drug-free lifestyle as an active and contributing member of society'* (Scottish Government, 2008).

What all three definitions have in common is a basic assumption of three properties or characteristics; two of them are observable – abstinence and some form of active participation in society, and one of them is experiential – well-being and life quality.

Is there anything problematic with these definitions?

To illustrate why the three definitions are problematic, we need to refer to the mental health recovery arena. Pat Deegan, a respected writer and expert by experience, defines recovery in a slightly different way. She argues that: *'Recovery refers to the lived experience of people as they accept and overcome the challenge of disability ... they experience themselves as recovering a new sense of self and of purpose within and beyond the limits of the disability'* (Deegan, 1998).

There are two key variations in Deegan's definition: the first is the emphasis on the experiential rather than the observable – in other words, the subjective is emphasised as central – and the second variation is the supposition that recovery does not require the remission of symptoms. In the course of research work, the author has gathered around 1,000 recovery stories and on reading them, two things become immediately apparent. First, there is very little that recovery journeys have in common, so distilling common factors is problematic. Second, for most people recovery is experienced as a process rather than as a state. Combined, these factors suggest that definitions not only have to account for marked variability across individuals, but they also have to be able to incorporate substantial shifts over time within individuals.

Evidently, recovery is hard to capture in a simple definition. This is a blessing because it may not be useful to regard recovery as something that can be observed and characterised as a set of presenting criteria. If definitions of recovery should account for the ideas of transcendence of a disorder, and of an experiential state, we would not expect that it is readily recognised or pinned down. There is also a 'political' dimension to this plurality – recovery is something characterised by personal experiences, embedded in families and communities – and so it is not at all obvious that something that looks diagnostic is helpful or within the spirit of a recovery definition.

Consistent with this approach, the US Centre for Substance Abuse Treatment (CSAT) suggests that a definition is less useful than a series of principles. The CSAT characterises recovery using the following 12 principles.

1. There are many pathways to recovery.
2. Recovery is self-directed and empowering.

Addiction Recovery: A movement for social change and personal growth in the UK © Pavilion Publishing (Brighton) Ltd 2012

3. Recovery involves a personal recognition of the need for change and transformation.

4. Recovery is holistic.

5. Recovery has cultural dimensions.

6. Recovery exists on a continuum of improved health and well-being.

7. Recovery emerges from hope and gratitude.

8. Recovery involves a process of healing and self-redefinition.

9. Recovery involves addressing discrimination and transcending shame and stigma.

10. Recovery is supported by peers and allies.

11. Recovery involves rejoining and rebuilding a life in the community.

12. Recovery is a reality. (CSAT, 2009)

In the CSAT's principles the idea of recovery as a personal experience is key, as is the idea that it is an empowering and personal process that involves significant life changes beyond substance use. The CSAT document goes on to make a claim that will at first seem incredibly positive and optimistic. It states that, by the best summary of evidence available, 58% of people who have a lifetime of substance dependence will eventually recover. The paths to recovery are discussed in depth in Chapters 3–6 and it is important at this stage to differentiate between recovery as a way of moving on with life from recovery as a 'cure', which may or may not result from a recovery experience.

The final word on the subject of definitions goes to Philip Valentine who, in a chapter describing the establishment of the Connecticut Community for Addiction Recovery (CCAR), agreed the principle that 'You are in recovery if you say you are'. This is based on the idea that 'Who determines if a person is in recovery? The person in recovery' (Valentine, 2011, p264). Valentine goes on to describe the success the principle has brought in terms of empowerment and by avoiding unhelpful debates about the length of clean time and external judgments of functioning.

In this book there is no set definition of recovery but it is about developing a sense of purpose and meaning, quality of life and a sense of belonging.

What does this mean for research, policy and treatment?

The personal and individual quality of recovery as an experience and the general experience which reports that it is an ongoing process should provide a caveat for both policymakers and researchers, but does not resolve the question of assessment and measurement. Whether for commissioners in purchasing services, or for researchers attempting to quantify, the problem of 'operationalisation' persists – particularly where there may not be the opportunity to ask individuals whether they see themselves as being in recovery or where there may be grounds for concern about the answers given to such a question.

From the mental health field, Warner (2010) suggests that one operational measure is 'social recovery', by which 'in recovery' means living independently and engaging in meaningful activities in the community. This sense of purpose and belonging is central to the definition, although this will vary according to where people are in their recovery journey. For policymakers, this is a much harder question where experiential components – such as quality of life or a sense of meaning – are hard to measure and there is a quest for 'hard' indicators. For policymakers in the UK, the dominance of an experiential component has been implicit in the definitions of recovery.

In Scotland it has taken the form of: *'a process through which an individual is enabled to move from their problem drug use, towards a drug-free lifestyle as an active and contributing member of society'* (Scottish Government, 2008, p23). The 2010 UK strategy sets an aim that: *'The goal of all treatment is for drug users to achieve abstinence from their drug – or drugs – of dependency. In order to deliver against all the treatment system actions in the drug strategy, partnerships will recognise the need to have recovery as the bedrock of all commissioning decisions'* (HM Government, 2010, p20). While the UK strategy is set against a context of localism, neither the Scottish or the English drug strategy identifies clear targets for the strategic vision; both emphasise 'a drug-free' or 'abstinent' lifestyle and there is a similar commitment towards a meaningful and productive life. While the measurement of success remains unclear, it appears that 'operationalisations' of recovery targets will include a combination of:

- desistance from offending
- active engagement with family and effective parenting
- meaningful activities and reduction in reliance on state benefits

- improvements in physical and psychological health

- evidence of abstinence from at least heroin and crack cocaine.

The origins of a 'recovery' movement in mental health

While many of the subsequent chapters focus on what research says about recovery from addiction, it is worth examining mental health as a parallel field that had some traction in establishing the concept of recovery. As, in addition to its contribution to definitions, experiences from the mental health arena have led the way in identifying the spirit of recovery and the principles associated with it.

Deegan (1993) argues that: *'Recovery is a process, not an endpoint or destination. Recovery is an attitude, a way of approaching the day and the challenges I face ... I know I have certain limitations and things I can't do. But rather than letting these limitations be occasions for despair and giving up, I have learned that in knowing what I can't do, I also open up the possibilities of all I can do.'* (Deegan, 1993, p7)

Davidson and Strauss (1992) note four stages in a personal recovery journey.

1. Discovering the possibility of taking ownership and responsibility.

2. Taking stock of one's strengths and limitations.

3. Putting aspects of the self into action.

4. Using this enhanced sense of self as a resource in recovery.

In both definitions there is a crucial recognition that recovery is not about remission or 'cure' but about transcending the symptoms and experience of mental health problems and focusing on strengths to live life to the full. This is very deliberately set against and in contrast to the goals of mental health treatment, where treatment stands for managing symptoms while recovery is about living a meaningful life. As Repper and Perkins argue: *'Recovery is not a professional intervention, like medication or therapy, and mental health workers do not hold the key. Many people have described the enormous support they have received from others who have faced a similar challenge...'* (Repper & Perkins, 2003, p47).

Repper and Perkins (2003) argue that there are some basic principles for professionals in working in a recovery-oriented way. These include developing hope-inspiring relationships; facilitating personal adaptation including understanding, acceptance and taking back control; and promoting inclusion and helping people access the roles and activities that are important to them. At the heart of this model is a sense of empowerment and control over life connected to a sense of belonging and purpose. This leads to a significant change in the role of the professional, as Slade (2009, p140) argues: *'The goal of mental health services is more explicitly the promotion and support of personal recovery. Clinical recovery has value, as one approach to supporting personal recovery. However, a primary focus on personal recovery would fundamentally change the values, goals and working practices of mental health services.'*

The supporting evidence for a recovery model in mental health

The evidence supporting the recovery model in mental health comes from a number of longitudinal studies. Harding *et al* (1987) conducted a 32-year follow-up study of the most difficult-to-place third of a population of psychiatric inpatient residents. At the follow-up point 81% were able to look after themselves, 25% were fully recovered and 41% showed significant improvements, while only 11% of people with severe and enduring mental illness did not show any improvement and remained within the treatment and support system. More recently, Warner (2010) reviewed the evidence of recovery and reported, from over 100 studies, that 20% of schizophrenics make a complete recovery and 40% make a 'social recovery' (defined as economic and residential independence and low social disruption), with work and empowerment being two of the key features of the recovery process.

Warner's study is particularly important as it suggests a multi-level approach to addressing recovery in specialist services that has echoes for the debate about abstinence in the addictions area. While it is likely that for many people recovery will require complete abstinence, this may be a long-term goal and there will be others who achieve their goals while remaining on medication and actively engaged with a range of helping services. The argument will be advanced in this book that for most people abstinence will be necessary and the most effective means of achieving social recovery is via abstinence-oriented approaches.

The recovery approach has led to marked changes not only in what outcomes are measured but also in what the aspirations and expectations are for clients, their family members and wider society. It has also led to changes in the commitment to empowerment and engagement that is common to mental health and addiction recovery, which creates a model of hope and activity that can challenge stereotypes and stigmatised perceptions. The recovery model that will be presented in the subsequent chapters will focus on the 'embedding' of recovery – embedding in the sense that it involves a sense of engagement and activity with the local community but also that it is likely to influence that community and 'give something back' as part of the recovery journey and process. However, this is not something new. Recovery is an organising concept and an increasingly recognisable set of shared values and beliefs, and much of what is presented will be familiar not only to those in recovery but also to workers and commissioners.

Chapter 2 focuses on the history of the international addiction recovery movement with a particular emphasis on mutual aid. The rich history of the key fellowship organisations – Alcoholics Anonymous, Narcotics Anonymous and Cocaine Anonymous – are outlined along with SMART Recovery. The emphasis is on the role they play in the UK recovery movement and how that is likely to evolve in the coming months and years, and how these relate to the current picture of communities of recovery. There is also a brief consideration of the role of treatment services in supporting or blocking the mutual aid movement.

Chapter 3 addresses the question 'What are the principles of recovery?'. It outlines the question of who recovers, when and why, by drawing on a research evidence base from both the UK and internationally, and examining recovery among those who access formal supports and treatment, and those who do not. The concept of 'recovery capital' as the currency of recovery is introduced in this chapter and examined as a way of assessing where people are in their recovery journey. The overall hypothesis of the nature of recovery is outlined, linking the ideas of recovery capital with developmental process and growth.

Chapter 4 examines the rates of recovery. It starts with a review of what is known about 'natural recovery' and what enables people to make lasting changes without engaging with a formal treatment service. It then examines longitudinal recovery studies from the US and the UK and studies of recovered populations describing their own stories and experiences. This draws heavily on recent recovery studies in Glasgow and Birmingham, and also discusses the findings that, for some people, recovery is not about 'going back' to where they were before their addiction and subsequent recovery, but about 'going beyond' and experiencing life in a different and more fulfilling way.

In Chapter 5 the focus switches to the relationship between treatment and recovery. In particular, it examines the transition from what William White (2008) referred to as the 'acute approach' to a developmental or continuing care model. The evidence from long-term treatment studies is considered but the primary focus is on the role that treatment services can play in developing recovery models and approaches. This relies heavily on the role of the worker as a therapeutic agent of change and as a bridge to communities of recovery. There is some consideration of the role of structures and systems within treatment services, but the focus is on the interpersonal work done by staff in enabling and managing the change process.

The rationale for this focus on interpersonal approaches is made explicit in Chapter 6, which examines the notion that recovery is fundamentally a social process. Drawing on evidence from the Framingham Heart Study, the emphasis is on the central role of peer selection and peer influence in establishing what is possible and how the world is understood (Christakis & Fowler, 2006). Much of the evidence presented focuses on the possibility of facilitating and sustaining the transition from social networks of fellow users to social networks consisting of people in active recovery. The final section of the chapter completes the model of how recovery is a socially embedded process that enables the development of both personal resources (such as self-esteem and a positive identity) and community supports (including access to visible recovery champions).

In the following chapters, the focus switches to what has been achieved in the UK, both at a national level and in terms of the growing recovery communities in particular cities. Chapter 7 reviews the national policies in England and Scotland and considers the opportunities they have afforded innovative practice. The commitment at national level to both the language and philosophy of recovery has set a major challenge for commissioners and service providers and one of the questions this chapter attempts to address is 'Why are policy makers so committed to a recovery model?', often in the face of opposition from a number of policy advisers and experts.

Addiction Recovery: A movement for social change and personal growth in the UK ©
Pavilion Publishing (Brighton) Ltd 2012

Chapter 8 starts with an overview of the evidence available for effective recovery-oriented systems of care and what lessons can be learned from attempts at 'system transformation' in the US. A UK example is considered, with a focus on Edinburgh. The chapter characterises what makes Edinburgh a recovery city, based around a number of key hubs – in particular the emergence of a quasi-residential rehabilitation and the emergence of a vibrant recovery community, characterised by the growth of mutual aid meetings in the city and the emergence of the Serenity Café, as a celebration of recovery in Edinburgh.

Chapter 9 looks at Yorkshire and Humberside and attempts to initiate recovery-oriented systems of care in the city. The wider systems approach is considered and attempts at 'commissioning recovery systems' is reviewed in the context of generating community activity and attempts at changing the workforce. In Chapter 10 the focus switches to northwest England and considers the emergence of 'indigenous' communities of recovery and, in particular, peer activities to generate recovery communities. It considers the example of Liverpool, which has had a relatively long-standing recovery model, and assesses the impact in other parts of the northwest.

The final chapters in the book begin to draw together the key themes that are emerging. The aim of Chapter 11 is to review models for success and learning from across the UK of what works in recovery. It attempts to draw together the lessons from natural, emerging recovery groups and communities with attempts at system change by commissioners and service providers and to assess what the overall picture is for attempting to implement the national strategies outlined at the start of the chapter.

Finally, in Chapter 12 some tentative overall conclusions about future directions are reached and framed in terms of an overall model of recovery capital and what communities and treatment providers can do to support and sustain this. It also sets out some of the challenges likely to be faced in the coming months and years.

Conclusion

In a presidential proclamation in 2009, Barack Obama paid tribute to recovery month and asserted the state's commitment to recovery in the US. He said: *'The journey to recovery requires great fortitude and a supportive network. As we celebrate National Alcohol and Drug Addiction Recovery Month, we also express our appreciation for the family members, mutual aid groups, peer support programmes, health professionals, and community leaders that provide compassion, care, and hope. Across the US, we must spread the word that substance abuse is preventable, that addiction is treatable, and that recovery is possible'* (Obama, 2010).

In the UK, both the English and Scottish governments have paved the way for an equally vibrant and successful model of recovery, but its delivery is not guaranteed and will require leadership, strategic vision and the delivery of successes that are visible and recognisable to policymakers, practitioners and communities. This handbook sets out the early tentative steps of a 'recovery movement' that is evidence-based and will set a model for developing a recovery framework for the UK.

Key learning points

■ Recovery is a process rather than an event and it is often characterised as a journey. Recovery is individual and personal, with the duration and nature of it varying across people and settings.

■ However, this does not mean that it is entirely unpredictable and there are patterns and sequences strong enough to make it worthy of scientific study.

■ Recovery is social in nature with recovery journeys involving other people and taking place in social settings.

■ Recovery is also a social movement of change that helps to build and transform local communities.

References

Betty Ford Institute Consensus Panel (2007) What is recovery? A working definition from the Betty Ford Institute. *Journal of Substance Abuse Treatment* **33** 221–228.

Centre for Substance Abuse Treatment (2009) *Guiding Principles and Elements of Recovery Orientated Systems of Care: What do we know from the research?* Rockville, MD: Substance Abuse and Mental Health Services Administration.

Christakis N & Fowler J (2009) *Connected: The surprising power of our social networks and how they shape our lives.* New York: Little, Brown and Company.

Davidson L & Strauss J (1992) Sense of self in recovery from severe mental illness. *British Journal of Medical Psychology* **65** 131–145.

Deegan P (1993) Recovering our sense of value after being labelled mentally ill. *Journal of Psychosocial Nursing and Mental Health* **31** 7–11.

Deegan P (1998) Recovery: the lived experience of rehabilitation. *Psychosocial Rehabilitation Journal* **11** 11–19.

Harding C, Brooks G, Ashikage T, Strauss J & Brier A (1987) The Vermont longitudinal study of persons with severe mental illness II: long-term outcomes of subjects who retrospectively met DSM-III criteria for schizophrenia. *The US Journal of Psychiatry* **144** 727–735.

HM Government (2010) *Drug Strategy 2010: Restricting demand, reducing supply, building recovery.* London: Home Office.

Obama B (2010) Presidential Proclamation for National Alcohol and Drug Addiction Recovery Month.

Repper J & Perkins R (2003) *Social Inclusion and Recovery: A model for mental health practice.* London: Balliere Tindall.

Scottish Government (2008) *The Road to Recovery.* Edinburgh: The Scottish Government.

Slade M (2009) *Personal Recovery and Mental Illness: A guide for health professionals.* Cambridge: Cambridge University Press.

UK Drug Policy Commission (2008) *The UK Drug Policy Commission Recovery Consensus Group: A vision of recovery.* London: UK Drug Policy Commission.

Valentine P (2011) Peer-based recovery support services within a recovery community organisation: The CCAR experience. In: J Kelly & W White (Eds) *Addiction Recovery Management: Theory, research and practice.* Springer, New York: Humana Press.

Warner R (2010) Does the scientific evidence support the recovery model? *The Psychiatrist* **34** 3–5.

White W (2008) *Recovery Management and Recovery-oriented Systems of Care: Scientific rationale and promising practices.* Pittsburgh, PA: Northeast Addiction Technology Transfer Center, Great Lakes Addiction Technology Transfer Center, Philadelphia Department of Behavioural Health and Mental Retardation Services.

Chapter 2

Mutual aid and the history of the addiction recovery movement

A comprehensive history of the US recovery movement can be found in William Whites *Slaying the Dragon: The history of addiction treatment and recovery in America*. The early chapters of the book outline the birth of the concept of alcoholism as a disease using the work of Benjamin Rush in the late 18th century, and this is tracked through to the emergence of the temperance movement in the early 19th century. However, the first indications of interventions related to alcohol are associated with the recognition of 'alcoholic psychoses' in the period between 1819 and 1831, which were largely managed with asylums before the appearance of the first inebriate homes (White attributes this to the launch of the US Association for the Care of Inebriates in 1870). From 1840 onwards, White describes the emergence of physical treatments for alcohol treatment, which preceded a glut of drug therapies, 'natural therapies' and surgical interventions.

The earliest emergence of treatment for narcotics and other drugs is described by White as beginning in the US in 1880. He characterised the late 19th century as one of stigmatisation in which opiate use was largely 'hidden' and so seeking treatment was generally seen as a last resort. However, the key event was legislative with the Harrison Anti-Narcotic Act, passed in 1914, which represented a transition from uncontrolled access to access regulated by physicians, which transpired to require reducing doses of prescription narcotic drugs. Increasingly, White argues, illicit drug use was associated with 'undesirables' and increasing legal sanctions were brought to bear against clinicians involved in prescribing drugs to addicts. White goes on to describe the treatment of drug addiction in the period between 1925 and 1950 as increasingly punitive and linked to the criminal justice system. This period was characterised by the opening of two 'narcotic farms' in Texas and Kentucky in the 1930s, which were seen as mechanisms of 'quarantine' for drug addicts. It is against this increasing disjunction in the management of alcohol and drug addiction that the most prominent of the mutual aid groups emerged – Alcoholics Anonymous (AA).

The story of the birth of AA has been told widely. The initial meeting between Bill Wilson and Dr Bob Smith took place in Akron, Ohio, in 1935, and the first publication of *The Big Book* came in 1939. The growth of AA was rapid, reaching 100 members in 1939 and by the 1950s membership had exceeded 90,000 (White, 1998). However, White is keen to point out that there were many embryonic mutual aid organisations that preceded AA, including the Washingtonian Movement and the Oxford Group, but it is AA that is synonymous with the emergence of mutual aid in the alcohol field, and subsequently the emergence of parallel organisations to address issues as diverse as heroin addiction, gambling addiction and over-eating. Its central tenets – identification and hope, proscriptions for daily living and mutual support – are critical to a much wider definition of recovery activities. The application of the AA programme to heroin addiction is dated by White as emerging between 1947 and 1953, and was originally named Addicts Anonymous. AA and Narcotics Anonymous (NA) have evolved significantly since those early days and are characterised by diversity, both in the US and the UK.

What is the evidence for the effectiveness of AA, NA and other mutual aid organisations?

A good source of evidence is *Circles of Recovery* (2004) by Keith Humphreys. The book sets out not only a growing and supportive evidence base for AA but also for other mutual aid organisations including NA, Gamblers Anonymous (GA), Cocaine Anonymous (CA), SMART Recovery and Women for Sobriety (WFS). While much of the original evidence was based on cross-sectional evidence, there is an increasing evidence base from trial and longitudinal research. Perhaps the strongest support comes from Project MATCH Group (1998) in which a manualised version of AA (called Twelve Step Facilitation) was compared to and performed as well as two other manualised treatment interventions – motivational enhancement therapy and cognitive behavioural therapy.

Scientific studies regarding the effects of participation in recovery mutual aid societies on long-term recovery outcomes are limited in scope and methodological rigour, although the span and rigour have increased significantly in the past decade (Humphreys, 2006). Seen as a whole, mutual aid outcome studies conclude that participation in recovery mutual aid societies typically enhances long-term recovery rates, elevates global functioning, and reduces post-recovery costs to society among diverse demographic and clinical populations (Kelly & Yeterian, 2008; White, 2009). In their review of the evidence base for the Scottish Government, Best *et al* (2010) conclude that: '*The effects of recovery mutual aid involvement are interdependent with the timing, frequency, intensity, and duration of involvement. For clients in addiction treatment, affiliation with and benefits from recovery mutual aid societies are influenced by counsellor attitudes toward mutual aid, the style of linkage (assertive versus passive, degree of choice, and personal matching), and the timing of linkage (during treatment versus following treatment)*' (Best *et al*, 2010, p36).

There is also increasing evidence that post-treatment engagement in mutual aid is of benefit for the children of substance-using parents. Andreas and O'Farrell (2009) reported on the impact of AA attendance after formal treatment on the psychiatric well-being of children with alcoholic fathers, as outlined above and discussed in Chapter 6: Recovery, social networks and contagion. They found that fathers' greater involvement in AA groups predicted children's lower externalising problems. Similarly, Callan and Jackson (1985) assessed adolescent children of recovering alcoholics in Queensland and found that the children of fathers in long-term recovery from drinking rated their families as happier, more cohesive, more trusting and more affectionate than families where the fathers still drank.

Within the model put forward in this book, Putnam (2000) suggests that around two per cent of the population in the US is active in some form of mutual aid or self-help group – and that these provide invaluable emotional support and interpersonal ties. In a work that documents the decline in membership of formal organisations in the US, Putnam argues that the growth of the mutual aid movement has been one of the crucial developments that has enabled social capital to be maintained in communities. In other words, it is the growth of mutual aid that has provided a sense of belonging and identity for people who would otherwise be disenfranchised in their communities.

What are the key lessons to learn from the mutual aid research?

Two of the most important lessons come from recent studies; the first is a study of network support in which clinicians attempted to engage individuals with recovery support via mutual aid groups (Litt *et al,* 2007). In a trial assessing the impact of 'network support', when compared to standard case management approaches, Litt *et al* (2007) found that the addition of one clean and sober individual to the social network reduced relapse rates in drinkers by 27% in the following year. The network support in this study involved linkage to AA groups and this yielded the clean and sober peers that were found to be an essential predictor of ongoing abstinence. While the impact of social networks is discussed in more detail in Chapter 6, the crucial lesson from Litt's work is that changing social networks does not have to be a part of 'maturing out' and that it can be supported and encouraged by clinicians or peers as a protective form of intervention.

There has also been considerable work since Project MATCH on interventions to make mutual aid groups more accessible. Timko *et al* (2005) conducted a randomised control trial to compare a 'standard' and 'intensive' referral intervention to encourage 12-step meeting attendance among substance misusing outpatients. At six months, those in the intensive referral condition showed significantly greater 12-step involvement (for example, they accessed a provided service, experienced a spiritual awakening and currently had a sponsor) and achieved significantly better substance use outcomes. Tonigan *et al* (2003) reported a fourfold reduction in relapse rates among AA members who had a sponsor compared to those who did not. This study – supporting the idea of 'assertive linkage' as the way of actively engaging people with community groups – has ramifications for activities outside of mutual aid (see Chapter 6 for a further discussion). A second initiative (Subbaraman *et al*, 2011) presented findings from the Making Alcoholics Anonymous Easier programme showing that not only does this form of assertive intervention increase the likelihood of abstinence, but that more active engagement in AA (by 'doing service' or by having a sponsor) also increased the effects of the intervention. In other words, there are things that can be done to actively engage individuals who are ambivalent and to allow us to move beyond the position of accepting passively that mutual aid groups 'aren't for everyone'.

12-step fellowships in the UK

In the UK, AA meetings have grown from the first meeting in 1947 to more than 4,300 local groups. Other 12-step groups have also spread throughout the UK, with more than 600 local NA meetings (Lopez Gaston *et al*, 2010), and at the time of writing there are around 800 meetings listed on the NA website. CA groups are also rapidly growing in the UK.

A recent survey in the UK indicated that in 2011 there were approximately 4,600 AA meetings, 896 NA meetings, 90 Al-Anon meetings, 242 CA meetings and 88 SMART Recovery meetings (McCartney, personal communication).

Christo & Franey (1995) found that increased NA attendance was associated with improved self-esteem and reduced anxiety. In surveys conducted in residential treatment settings in south London, Best *et al* (2001) found that the group format and the focus on spirituality was a significant barrier for a proportion of drinkers and drug users. Illicit drug users were typically more positive about attending meetings during their inpatient stay and were more likely to attend meetings after their departure from the unit. In follow-up research on the alcohol cohort from this initial survey, Gossop *et al* (2003) found that more frequent AA attendance following inpatient treatment was associated with better drinking outcomes, but did not lead to significantly greater improvements in other measures of functioning relative to those who attended fewer AA meetings.

However, cultural issues persist. Day *et al* (2005) explored barriers to accessing 12-step meetings in statutory addiction treatment clients by assessing the opinions of treatment staff. In a survey of 346 workers, less than half (46%) recommended that their clients attend AA or NA meetings, with workers from non-nursing backgrounds particularly unlikely to encourage 12-step meeting attendance. The view of many workers that addiction is a 'bad habit' rather than a disease was a deterrent to actively encouraging clients to attend 12-step meetings. Day *et al* (2005) concluded that there were fundamental differences in the receptiveness to the 12-step philosophy in the UK relative to the US. There are two major dangers with this separation and division into silos of 'treatment' and mutual aid. First, that users of treatment services do not have the opportunity to experience the benefits outlined above, and second, there is a significant danger of service users not being aware of those who have achieved and sustained recovery.

This is described as a 'social learning' model in which one of the crucial benefits of engagement in recovery groups and communities is the opportunity to observe and imitate the successful behaviours and practices of those individuals who have progressed further in their recovery journeys (Moos, 2001). White (2008) has outlined a number of major benefits of engaging in recovery groups, several of which reflect this basic mechanism of social learning. They are:

- experience of acceptance and belonging
- building esteem through identification with a large organisation
- providing a belief system through which shame and defeat can be transformed into victory
- providing a vehicle for the safe discharge of powerful emotions
- providing a consistent set of rituals that facilitate emotional release and value-focusing
- providing a forum for consultation on daily problem-solving
- providing rituals that allow the group to celebrate success.

There is a concern among some treatment professionals – as outlined in Day *et al*'s (2005) study and further examined by Best *et al* (2010) – that workers see 12-step groups as a form of cult that may put clients at risk and are suitable only for those with strong religious beliefs who have already achieved and sustained abstinence. 12-step groups will vary markedly in their activities and mechanisms and it is the social learning component combined with a sense of belonging and purpose that may be critical. While other kinds of recovery groups are discussed below, the strongest evidence base has been developed around the 12-step fellowships and workers in specialist addiction treatment should at least attend one open meeting before making any decisions about their willingness to refer clients to these groups.

Other forms of mutual aid

While there is strong supporting evidence in favour of the fellowships, there is a number of clients who will not be willing to engage and this should not mean that they are denied the benefits of mutual aid group attendance described previously. In the UK, the most accessible form of such an alternative is SMART Recovery. There are three types of recovery support that are particularly relevant to the recovery journey.

- Recovery mutual aid groups – including AA, NA, CA, SMART and other groups of individuals in abstinent or maintained recovery – but the purpose of the group is explicitly to maintain one another's recovery.

Addiction Recovery: A movement for social change and personal growth in the UK © Pavilion Publishing (Brighton) Ltd 2012

- Vocational groups – this will include projects targeting education and training, but will also include volunteering projects and other initiatives where groups of people in recovery meet to support and develop their interests and skills.

- Interest groups – this will be more typically sport or hobby groups such as football teams, hill-walking clubs or dramatic arts such as music evenings and theatre groups.

While clients may benefit from shopping around, many do not feel the need to stick to one group and may attend a range of mutual aid groups and other community supports to fulfil different parts of their recovery journeys at different times – thus it is not a case of AA or SMART, NA or volunteering groups, but of linking people in recovery to a range of supportive activities they can engage with to meet different and often complementary needs. If the client does want to go to 12-step groups, it might also be useful to ask if their partner or family members would be interested in Al-Anon or other family support groups. The chapters on recovery in the UK describe some of the innovative recovery projects that have been undertaken and flourished, but the basic premise is that the increased availability of diverse options of mutual support – for people at different stages of their recovery journeys and to cater to different needs – will be essential in enabling the 'empowerment' and 'belonging' components of recovery process for most people.

White (2008) argues that the core social functions of recovery groups are:

- emotional support – involving empathy, care, consideration, concern and encouragement

- informational support – providing knowledge about recovery and the recovery support services and groups available

- instrumental support – support in linking in to supportive housing and childcare services, development of leisure and sporting activities and to recovery groups

- companionship

- validation – sharing and supporting their recovery experiences.

What is the future of recovery groups in the UK?

There is already an increasing diversity of recovery groups from the more formal and therapeutic to informal and occasional alliances of people who come together for specific purposes. We should not aim to be prescriptive about what should be available in any area – that should be driven by the interests, skills and needs of people at different stages of their recovery journeys. One of the core challenges, however, will be to address the recovery needs of those engaged in long-term opioid substitution prescribing. McKeganey (2011) cites data from the National Treatment Agency for Substance Misuse in England showing that in 2007/08, 146,999 people were in receipt of a methadone prescription, and that there are around 22,000 individuals in Scotland on methadone prescriptions. While the issues around methadone are discussed in Chapter 5, a comprehensive recovery community must offer attractive options to this vast group of people and offer ways of mobilising shared activities and shared support among maintained populations of users. This does not mean groups run by professionals that clients are invited or required to attend, but peer-based activities that enable and promote recovery.

From the perspective of commissioning and enabling communities of recovery, there is an initial challenge – that is, the concern that the 'vital elements' of recovery communities will be lost once there is too much professional interference and that the groups will not actively engage recovering communities because they are seen as little more than adjuncts to professional treatment. The experience in parts of west Scotland with attempting to enable SMART recovery groups by initiating them through professional services – with the aim of handing them over – was not as successful as hoped because of problems with empowerment and hand-over. This does not mean that there are no roles for professionals but there must be strong enough drives to have the group in the first place from some individuals undertaking recovery journeys and clear enough peer ownership of the group. This may necessitate locating the meetings away from specialist treatment agencies, having 'closed' components of meetings where only peers are in attendance or by having a committee or board with only peers as members.

A treatment provider or commissioner can enable, empower and support – whether this takes the form of providing financial or expert assistance with set-up costs and activities, specialist knowledge, such as accessing information about social enterprise or Community Interest Companies

(CIC), and offering training and support to those establishing the group – including basic awareness of issues around clinical supervision, business planning and so on. However, as with specialist workers and recovery groups, what services and commissioners can most usefully do is to act as a bridge to a range of populations and groups – potential members of the recovery groups, peers and equivalents from other areas, community members and representatives, and also to 'sell' the group to specialist staff and services who will be key referrers and beneficiaries of the group. There is no automatic assumption that this help will be needed (the 12-step fellowships have flourished in its absence), but it may well provide the necessary lift to get things moving and to provide the 'stabilisers' while the core group are learning to take control.

It will be equally important to ensure that the recovery groups do not exist in a 'silo' that is outside the treatment system, and so potentially starved of funding opportunities, links to shared resources – training, IT and so on – and to the clients in treatment services who may provide the core membership. Although a recovery-oriented system of care should have flexibility, those setting up a group and those attempting to support it should have some idea where it sits in relation to the specialist providers and to make sure that appropriate linkages are developed. Recovery communities will not operate by the same rules as specialist providers – and will need to make decisions about management and governance – but these should be clear to reassure specialist services that their clients will not be at risk. All of the issues of 'assertive linkage' will apply to ensuring that treatment staff are reassured, understand what the group is for and will provide encouragement and support to their clients to attend and engage.

Conclusion

Recovery does not occur in treatment although treatment may be both a catalyst and a prerequisite for some people. Nevertheless, as White (2008) argues, it will typically be more than five years after the last drink and between five and seven years after the last use of heroin that the person can regard their recovery as stable (but not guaranteed). For this reason, enabling recovery in communities is an essential part of protecting, where possible, those long-term aspects of recovery that will not involve acute specialist care. From a recovery systems model, it is not satisfactory to rely on people to find their way to the mutual aid groups that may or may not exist in their neighbourhood, village or town. For this reason, it is incumbent on addiction professionals not only to know about the community resources available, but to enable and support them wherever possible.

One of the core challenges for the emerging 'recovery movement' in the UK is to achieve three things.

1. Generate an increasing awareness among professional staff and services in specialist agencies of the vital role of communities and recovery groups, to embrace, engage, 'bridge' and support nascent and established recovery communities.

2. Enable and empower people in recovery to engage with existing groups, to utilise their interests and skills to establish new groups – therapeutic, vocational or interest-based – and provide support and guidance on how to sustain such groups as an active vibrant part of a wider recovery network and a visible celebration of recovery in the lived community.

3. Create a forum for information exchange and understanding among those actively involved in recovery groups and communities to develop a suitable style of evidence base for recovery groups in the UK. This will rarely take the form of randomised trial research but will create a framework for meaningful standards and for actively engaging local services.

Recovery is a personal journey of transformation and hope; one that is embedded in a sense of belonging and meaning, to families, groups and the community. Recovery groups in the UK already capture the remarkable diversity and range of personal recovery pathways and it is the capacity to support and enable them without stifling their unique peer-based and community focus that will determine the success in generating recovery-oriented systems in the UK.

Key learning points

■ There is a strong and supportive evidence base for attending mutual aid groups based on solid scientific evidence.

■ Evidence shows that people who attend AA will have better outcomes in relation to drinking, and that the more engaged in groups they are, the better the outcome.

- There are barriers to engagement for some clients that include, on occasion, negative attitudes among professional staff.

- Nonetheless, the number of meetings in the UK continues to grow and is increasingly linked to recovery groups and communities.

- The recovery movement in the UK has largely been based on ground level activity supported by a growing network of national support groups and organisations.

References

Andreas J & O'Farrel T (2009) Alcoholics Anonymous attendance following 12-step treatment participation as a link between alcohol-dependent fathers' treatment involvement and their children's externalising problems. *Addiction* **36** 87–100.

Best D, Harris J, Gossop M, Manning V, Man LH, Marshall J, Bearn J & Strang J (2001) Are the twelve steps more acceptable to drug users than to drinkers? *European Addiction Research* **7** 69–77.

Best D, Rome A, Hanning K, White W, Gossop M, Taylor A & Perkins A (2010) *Research for Recovery: A review of the drugs evidence base*. Edinburgh: Scottish Government.

Callan V & Jackson D (1985) Children of alcohol fathers and recovered alcoholic fathers: personal and family functioning. *Journal of Studies on Alcohol* **47** (1) 180–182.

Christo G & Franey C (1995) Drug users' spiritual beliefs, locus of control and the disease concept in relation to Narcotics Anonymous attendance and six-month outcomes. *Drug and Alcohol Dependence* **38** 51–56.

Day E, Lopez Gaston R, Furlong E, Murali V & Copello A (2005) United Kingdom substance misuse workers' attitudes towards 12-step self help group. *Journal of Substance Abuse Treatment* 321–327.

Lopez Gaston R, Best D, Day E & White W (2010) Perceptions of 12-step interventions among UK substance misuse patients attending residential in-patient treatment in a UK treatment setting. *Journal of Groups in Addiction and Recovery* **5** 306–323.

Gossop M, Marsden J, Stewart D & Kidd T (2003) The National Treatment Outcome Research Study (NTORS): 4–5 year follow-up results. *Addiction* **98** 291–303.

Humphreys K (2004) *Circles of Recovery: Self-help organisations for addictions*. Cambridge: Cambridge University Press.

Humphreys K (2006) The trial of Alcoholics Anonymous. *Addiction* **101** 617–618.

Kelly J & Yeterian J (2008) Mutual-help groups. In: W O'Donohue & JR Cunningham (Eds) *Evidence-based Adjunctive Treatments*. New York: Elsevier.

Litt M, Kadden R, Kabela-Cormier E & Petry N (2007) Changing network support for drinking: Initial findings from the network support project. *Journal of Consulting and Clinical Psychology* **75** 542–555.

McKeganey N (2011) *Controversies in Drug Policy and Practice*. Basingstoke: Palgrave MacMillan.

Moos R (2001) Addictive disorders in context: principles and puzzles of effective treatment and recovery. *Psychology of Addictive Behaviours* **17** (1) 3–12.

Project MATCH Research Group (1998) Matching alcoholism treatments to client heterogeneity: Project MATCH three-year drinking outcomes. *Alcoholism: Clinical and Experimental Research* **22** (6) 1300–1311.

Putnam R (2000) *Bowling Alone: The collapse and revival of American community.* New York: Simon and Schuster.

Subbaraman M, Kaskutas L & Zemore S (2011, in press) Sponsorship and Service as mediators of the effects of Making Alcoholics Anonymous Easier (MAAEZ), a 12-step facilitation intervention. *Drug and Alcohol Dependence.*

Timko C, Dixon K & Moos R (2005) Treatment for dual diagnosis patients in the psychiatric and substance abuse systems. *Mental Health Services Research* **7** (4) 229–242.

Tonigan JS, Connors GJ & Miller WR (2003) Participation and involvement in Alcoholics Anonymous. In: TF Babor & FK Del Boca (Eds) *Treatment Matching in Alcoholism.* Cambridge: Cambridge University Press.

White WL (1998) *Slaying the Dragon: The history of addiction treatment and recovery in America.* Bloomington, Illinois: Chestnut Health Systems.

White W (2008) *Recovery Management and Recovery-Oriented Systems of Care: Scientific Rationale and Promising Practices.* Pittsburgh, PA: Northeast Addiction Technology Transfer Center, Great Lakes Addiction Technology Transfer Center, Philadelphia Department of Behavioural Health and Mental Retardation Services.

White W (2009) The mobilisation of community resources to support long-term addiction recovery. *Journal of Substance Abuse Treatment* **36** (2) 146–158.

Chapter 3

What are the principles of recovery?

Moving beyond definitions

The Centre for Substance Abuse Treatment (CSAT) suggests that principles of recovery may be more useful than a single definition (see Chapter 1). This is partly due to problems with establishing a consensual definition, and partly in recognition of the fact that recovery stories are so varied and are generally ongoing. However, this has not stopped the CSAT from summarising epidemiological, survey and outcome research to conclude that just over half of those with lifetime substance dependence will eventually achieve a meaningful recovery. This is generally based on the self-report of people who have taken part in outcome studies, population assessments or dedicated research projects examining recovery experiences or natural recovery, so there is no single definition.

Nonetheless, it is a crucial statement for those involved in the treatment, policy development and study of addiction and recovery as it challenges pessimism and misperceptions fuelled by the belief that addiction is a *'chronic, relapsing condition'* (O'Brien & McLellan, 1986). The fact that 58% of people achieve a meaningful recovery suggests that not only is recovery possible, it is probable (CSAT, 2009). More than half of those with a lifetime dependence will eventually recover. This does not imply that they will not have lapses and relapses, but that they will experience significant positive change. This chapter looks at how this happens with reference to the evidence base and links this to the concept of recovery capital. The final section of the chapter proposes a developmental model of recovery based on key life events and their relationship with the growth of recovery capital.

A brief excursion into the science of crime careers

The longitudinal study Shared Beginnings, Divergent Lives offers an incredible account of criminal careers (Laub & Sampson, 2003). The study attempted to address the question of the chronicity of offending – in other words, the proportion of young offenders who mature out of crime – and followed up a group of young offenders from Boston until the age of 70. Only a very small number of individuals persisted in their offending at the final research interview (when the offenders were on average aged 70) with the majority 'maturing out' of crime in their 30s and 40s. In this longitudinal cohort study, the long-term predictors of desistance of offending careers were:

- stable employment

- attachment to a conventional person (for example, a spouse)

- transformation of personal identity

- ageing

- inter-personal skills

- life and coping skills.

The study has provoked considerable debate about the significance of jobs and relationships, and whether they are markers of maturational change that has already taken place, or whether they are 'turning points' in themselves. Laub and Sampson (2003) argue that wives can act as 'social controllers' in preventing their husbands from mixing with deviant friends. Another important finding from the study was that the level of risk factors at the 'adolescent stage' had almost no predictive power around desistance. To address this finding, one can consider one of the most important UK longitudinal crime studies – the Cambridge Youth Study. In this study 411 boys born in a working class area of south London were interviewed at the ages of eight and 18, and then again at 32 and 48 (Farrington, 1995). Theobald and Farrington (2011) found that the protective effect of marriage – the reduction in offending in the five years after marriage compared to the five years before – only applied to those who married younger (for example, those who were 25 or older did not have this protective effect) and part of the reason for this was the role of alcohol and drugs. Theobald and Farrington suggest that *perhaps the taking of drugs and the continuation of binge drinking from adolescence to adulthood complicated the ability of the*

Addiction Recovery: A movement for social change and personal growth in the UK ©
Pavilion Publishing (Brighton) Ltd 2012

late-married men to reduce their offending behaviour, even if they were in stable marriages' (Theobald & Farrington, 2011, p152). The key conclusion from these studies is that there are developmental patterns of change but that these are influenced by life events.

Another longitudinal study of offending and substance use is the Ohio Life Course study. In this study participants incarcerated in youth institutions in 1985 were re-interviewed as adults in 1995 and 2003, when they were an average age of 29 and 38. Building on work on this cohort, which showed that high levels of adult criminal behaviour were linked to deviant peer networks and the criminality of partners, Schroeder *et al* (2007) split the cohort between 'desisters' (44.7%), 'persisters' (25.7%) and 'unstable offenders' (26.9%). Schroeder *et al* (2007) found that both alcohol and drug use were independently associated with persistent offending, but that the effects of drug use were stronger and more sustained. The study did not find that social bonds significantly mediated the relationship between substance use and criminality.

Applying a life-course model to the addictions field

In a 33-year outcome study conducted in the US, Hser *et al* (2007a; 2007b) found that self-efficacy and psychological well-being were predictors of stable recovery. One of their observations was that career pathways appeared to differ for different substances, with cocaine use increasing through the 20s to early 30s and then declining, but with heroin use continuing to increase. In terms of the typology of heroin users developed by Hser *et al* (2007a), the study differentiated between stable high-level users, decelerating users and early quitters. The last group (who constituted just under half of their longitudinal sample) had heroin careers of typically less than 10 years. This early quitting population of heroin users had higher frequencies of use in the first two to three years but then showed marked reductions and use was abstinent by year 11. Hser *et al* (2007b) emphasised key developmental concepts such as trajectories and turning points, although they conceded that there was a dearth of information about cessation factors.

It is also clear that there is typically a long time between initiation and eventual cessation. Dennis *et al* (2005) found that the median time from drug initiation to a full year of abstinence was 27 years, and the median time from first treatment to a year of abstinence was nine years and typically involved three to four episodes of treatment. Research from the same group showed transitions between the relapse, treatment re-entry and recovery cycles over a two-year period and found that 82% of the sample made at least one transition and 62% made multiple transitions (Scott *et al,* 2005). In other words, there may be long periods of ongoing addiction problems with frequent transitions in the cycle of treatment, relapse and recovery reported by Scott *et al* (2005).

In a more recent article, Teruya and Hser (2010) examined the concept of turning points in the life course and defined 'turning points' as *'particular events, experiences, or awareness that result in changes in the direction of a pattern or trajectory over the long term'* (Teruya & Hser, 2010, p2). The authors argue that turning points can only emerge in hindsight as a period of time must elapse before the stability of a change can be measured and identified. Teruya and Hser recognise that while some events are not predictable they are related to contextual factors, and comment that social resources and linkages can both inhibit and facilitate certain types of turning points. Indeed, Teruya and Hser (2010) cited Granfield and Cloud's (2001) study of 'natural recovery' as emphasising the role of turning points that involve other people (such as family responsibilities and death of parents) as well as dramatic events (such as imprisonment) that may cause a dramatic break with the environment the individual had faced prior to this point. Teruya and Hser (2001) emphasise the crucial experiential quality of a turning point – it is not the event itself but the impact the event has on the individual.

In their work on recovery journeys, outlined in *Beating the Dragon,* McIntosh and McKeganey (2000) describe 70 recovery experiences and conclude that the core transition to recovery is around the restoration of a 'spoiled identity'. Among the key desistance factors identified were developing new activities and relationships and developing a commitment towards new and changed lifestyles, at least in part by forming an identity as a non-addict. McIntosh and McKeganey (2000) identify two main mechanisms by which former users avoided relapse: *'(1) the avoidance of their former drug-using network and friends and (2) the development of a set of non-drug-related activities and relationships'* (McIntosh & McKeganey, 2000). The issues of social networks and the development of activities are critical to our understanding of recovery journeys.

In research on 205 individuals in recovery from alcohol and heroin addiction in Glasgow, the above factors were found to be critical in predicting quality of life in recovery (Best *et al,* 2011). The study also found that the more time spent with others in recovery, the better the recovery experience. It did not matter how much time the individuals spent with current users or with people who had never used substances problematically. The other major predictor of quality of life was activity. At the most basic level, the amount of time spent engaging in childcare, volunteering, group activities, training, education and employment was strongly linked to quality of life. In other words, the strongest predictors of life quality were engaging in a range of activities and doing so with other people also engaged in a recovery journey.

There is additional support for the intrinsically social nature of recovery from a UK study conducted by Best *et al* (2008). The study surveyed 107 former problematic heroin users who had achieved long-term abstinence and asked about their experiences of achieving and sustaining abstinence. The most commonly expressed reason for finally achieving abstinence was that they were 'tired of the lifestyle', followed by reasons relating to psychological health. In contrast, when asked to explain how abstinence was sustained, participants quoted social network factors (moving away from drug-using friends and support from non-using friends) and practical factors (accommodation and employment) as well as religious or spiritual factors. This social focus is further emphasised by Waldorf *et al* (1991), based on 267 in-depth interviews with heavy cocaine users. They found that many addicted people with supportive elements in their lives (a job, family, and other close emotional supports) were able to 'walk away' from their very heavy use of cocaine. Waldorf *et al* (1991) suggests that the 'social context' of drug users' lives might positively influence their ability to discontinue drug use. Biernacki (1986) reports on a range of strategies used in natural recovery, including:

■ breaking off relationships with other drug users

■ removing oneself from a drug-using environment

■ building new structures in one's life

■ using social networks of friends and family to provide support for the newly emerging recovery status.

Summarising the US evidence, White (2009) argues that there are four stages to a recovery journey.

1. Pre-recovery problem identification and internal/external resource mobilisation (destabilisation of addiction and recovery priming).

2. Recovery initiation and stabilisation, which will often include early interventions such as detoxification and substitute prescribing.

3. Recovery maintenance.

4. Enhancements and ongoing personal development and reintegration.

Within the mental health field, Rethink (2008) argues that there are three components of the first stage (resource mobilisation). The organisation states that before a recovery journey can meaningfully start, three conditions have to be in place. The person has to have a safe place to live that is free from threat; have basic human rights and choices; and be free from acute physical and psychiatric distress. From an addiction recovery model perspective, this implies that basic enablers of safety and 'breathing space' are needed before an individual can make a meaningful commitment to starting a recovery journey.

One of the core concepts of recovery is that ceasing to drink or use drugs is necessary but not sufficient. White and Kurtz (2006) argue that the period after cessation of substance use to 'stable' recovery is typically around five to seven years depending on the person's situation and supports. In this period there is likely to be increasing dissociation with the rituals and routines of the addict lifestyle and a switch in social networks away from those associated with active substance use. However, this is a complex path and there may well be slips and problems along the way. How recovery approaches differ from acute treatment models is in the assumption that the key areas for focus of attention and resource are in this five-year window, where the supports necessary are likely to be located in the family and the community, rather than in the specialist treatment provision.

What is recovery capital?

All the generalisations presented in this chapter should carry the ongoing health warning that recovery is a personal process and that individuals will vary in the style, stages and timings of their recovery. However, this does not mean that there is nothing to say about readiness for recovery. It is at this point that the language of recovery capital is particularly useful and important. Granfield and Cloud (2001) define recovery capital as *'the breadth and depth of internal and external resources that can be*

Addiction Recovery: A movement for social change and personal growth in the UK ©
Pavilion Publishing (Brighton) Ltd 2012

drawn upon to initiate and sustain recovery from AOD [alcohol and other drug] problems'. Granfield and Cloud argue that people who have access to greater reserves of recovery capital are better able to address problems than those who do not have such access. In the 2010 report on *Whole Person Recovery: A user-centred systems approach to problem drug use*, the Royal Society for the Arts outlined its core components of recovery capital as:

- housing
- physical and mental health
- purposeful activity: education, training and employment
- peer support
- family and friends

(RSA, 2010).

The basis for the recovery capital model was the conclusion reached by White and Cloud (2008) that the prediction of long-term recovery is more successful when based on assets and strengths rather than deficits. In Best and Laudet's (2010) model of recovery capital, there are essentially three component parts to recovery capital – personal capital, social capital and collective or community recovery capital.

Personal recovery capital: This refers to the skills, experiences and capabilities a person has. While it will include professional resources and skills such as qualifications and training courses, work experience and positive personal characteristics, it will also include the core enablers of self-esteem, self-efficacy, self-coping and a positive personal identity.

Social recovery capital: There is a considerable research literature on social capital from a range of academic traditions, but one of the texts most commonly cited in this respect is *Bowling Alone* by Robert Putnam (2000). Putnam defined social capital as *'Connections among individuals – social networks and the norms of reciprocity and trustworthiness that arise from them ... Social capital can [thus] be simultaneously a 'private good' and a 'public good'. Some of the benefits from an investment in social capital goes to bystanders, while some of the benefit rebounds to the immediate interest of the person making the investment'* (Putnam, 2000, p19–20). Thus, social capital is not simply a list of people; it is the shared investment and commitment between you and them, and the resulting resources and opportunities that arise.

Collective recovery capital: This is the attempt to identify and differentiate important aspects of community life that impact on the chances a person has in recovery, not least because of the overlap with social capital outlined above. The distinction, made by Best and Laudet (2010), is an attempt to differentiate the direct social networks of individuals with the broader context in which they live. Our model suggests that there are three context effects to social capital that are directly linked to recovery capital for addictive behaviours. In effect, these are the wider supports and resources that are available in the local community relating in turn to specialist treatment provision, the accessibility and attractiveness of recovery communities and champions, and the broader issues of opportunity and community safety.

These are:

- **Recovery capital and treatment:** As counsellors in specialist agencies can act as both inspiration and ally for raising expectancies that recovery is possible, and can support and enable key aspects of the recovery journey, the first contextual resource is the motivation and quality of staff in specialist treatment agencies, mediated by how accessible and attractive such treatment services are to those with addiction problems.

- **Recovery capital and champions:** While the issue of champions is addressed in much more detail in subsequent chapters, the second resource that a community can afford individuals starting a recovery journey is visible models of recovery, who are accessible and who model recovery as a reality that is appealing and meaningful for those in earlier stages of recovery progress. This is likely to be made manifest by their diversity and visibility, which is likely to involve some degree of formalisation through mutual aid and other groups.

- **Recovery capital and the lived community:** According to Rethink (2008), it is essential that some basic pre-conditions exist to enable a recovery journey – in particular, a safe place to live, some basic human rights and choices, and freedom from acute physical and psychiatric distress. Thus, there is an 'ecological' component to the probability of stable recovery that is influenced by access to safe and comfortable places to live, by the availability of jobs, courses and educational opportunities, and by the wider neighbourhood cohesion and participation.

A developmental recovery capital model of change

Attempting to quantify this model is complex as influences at each level can be either positive or negative. Cloud and Granfield (2009) discuss what they mean by 'negative recovery capital' – the adverse impact on a recovery journey of a history of mental health problems, significant prior engagement with the criminal justice system, and also potentially age and gender. How this would play out in a developmental model of recovery capital is that there are positive, negative and neutral influences on developmental trajectories of change, and that the impact of these events or experiences will be determined by the resources and supports (at all three levels) available to the individual. Chapter 6 argues that this process is intrinsically social and that the social capital component of recovery potential is central in both enabling recovery-supportive events and in and by increasing the impact on positive life changes.

While this model will be fleshed out in considerably more detail in subsequent chapters, some basic comments will be made in the remainder of this chapter about what this model implies for supporting and enabling change. The first and most important thing to say is that this is a developmental model and so key life events can be both positive and negative – thus, the birth of a child may increase positive personal and social capital but the loss of a job or the end of a positive relationship may well represent significant 'risk windows' for a relapse and return to substance use. This is part of the reason why nobody is ever 'safe' in their recovery – life events can disturb the stability of recovery and disrupt protective routines. The model suggests, however, that the combination of personal resources (such as positive self-esteem and a non-addict identity (Biernacki, 1986; McIntosh & McKeganey, 2000)), combined with supportive social networks of recovery can reduce the risk and potentially minimise the damage done to recovery journeys.

A finding from a meta-analysis of the effectiveness of mutual aid by Kyrouz and Humphreys (1997) is relevant. Conducting a meta-analysis of the key elements of mutual aid group attendance, Humphreys (2003) identified four factors – active coping, increased motivation to change, better friendship quality and friend support for abstinence. This model suggests that there is a complex dynamic of personal growth (coping skills and motivation) bound to changes in the type and quality of social networks. This is critical to the idea that much of recovery initiation may be based on the observation of others who are in recovery (social learning), learning of coping skills and techniques from them and becoming embedded in supportive networks that enable and support the growth and nurturing of these skills and resources. The importance of social networks for recovery is discussed in more detail in Chapter 6.

Conclusion

Any attempt at generating a model of recovery is ambitious and in danger of over-stretching our knowledge on recovery. Recovery is an individual process, which is experienced by the majority of people as an ongoing journey, and there is no point of ultimate 'safety' or stability beyond which there is no risk of relapse. These problems are compounded by the unpredictability of life events – both positive and negative – that can shift trajectories and, in one single action, cause an avalanche on the mountain that has been painstakingly scaled.

Nonetheless, there are the foundations for a developmental model predicated on the idea that there are fundamental enablers – a safe place to live, freedom from acute physical or psychiatric distress and basic choices – that create the opportunity to start a recovery journey. The basic currency of that journey is recovery capital, consisting of resources, ties, networks and opportunity, and the direction mediated by key life events that act as trajectory changes. Thus, whether getting married acts as a 'turning point' will depend on the existence of the basic enablers and the shift it may generate in both social ties and internal values and actions (motivation to abstain and active participation in recovery work). The potential role of treatment in enabling and supporting recovery journeys is explored in Chapter 5.

At this point, it would be an accepted academic convention to couch the above model in caveats about limited empirical support and a lack of appropriate research testing, but this is the initial exposition of a model. The subsequent chapters attempt to provide evidence, both gathered by the author and other sources, to support this model.

Key learning points

- As recovery is a process, a useful model to understanding recovery is in developmental terms and to think of recovery as a 'career'.

- This model introduces the idea of 'trajectories' that people progress along and 'turning points' that are the key events that can change the direction of people's lives.

- Some of these key events happen to everyone – new relationships, houses, bereavements – and the impact they have on people will depend on where they are and what resources they can draw on.

- That idea is referred to as 'recovery capital' – which is the basic 'currency' of measuring where someone is on their recovery journey.

- In the proposed model of recovery capital, there are three aspects to recovery capital – personal resources, social supports and the collective resources available in the local community.

- The model suggests that the likelihood of positive change depends on these factors coinciding with windows of opportunity for change.

References

Best, D, Ghufran, S, Day, E, Ray, R & Loaring J (2008) Breaking the habit: a retrospective analysis of desistance factors among formerly problematic heroin users. *Drug and Alcohol Review* **27** (6) 619–624.

Best D, Groshkova T, Sadler J, Day E & White W (2011) What is recovery? Functioning and recovery stories of self-identified people in recovery in a service users' group and their peer networks in Birmingham, England. *Alcoholism Treatment Quarterly* **29** 293–313.

Best D & Laudet A (2010) *The Potential for Recovery Capital.* London: Royal Society for the Arts.

Biernacki P (1986) *Pathways from Heroin Addiction Recovery without Treatment.* Philadelphia: Temple University Press.

Centre for Substance Abuse Treatment (2009) *Guiding Principles and Elements of Recovery-Oriented Systems of Care: What do we know from the research?* Rockville, MD: Centre for Substance Abuse Treatment.

Cloud W & Granfield W (2009) Conceptualising recovery capital: expansion of a theoretical construct. *Substance Use and Misuse* 42 (12/13) 1971–1986.

Dennis M, Scott C, Funk R & Foss M (2005) The duration and correlates of addiction and treatment careers. *Journal of Substance Abuse Treatment* **28** S51–S62.

Farrington D (1995) The development of offending and anti-social behaviour from childhood: Key findings from the Cambridge Study in delinquent development. *Journal of Child Psychology and Psychiatry* **36** 929–964.

Granfield R & Cloud W (2001) Social context and natural recovery: The role of social capital in the resolution of drug-related problems. *Substance Use and Misuse* **36** 1543–1570.

Hser Y-I (2007a) Predicting long-term stable recovery from heroin addiction: findings from a 33-Year follow-up study. *Journal of Addictive Diseases* **26** (1) 51–60.

Hser Y-I, Longshore D & Anglin MD (2007b) The life course perspective on drug use: a conceptual framework for understanding drug use trajectories. *Evaluation Review* **31** (6) 515–547.

Humphreys K (2003) Alcoholics Anonymous and 12-step alcoholism treatment programmes. *Recent Developments in Alcohol* **16** 149–164.

Kyrouz E & Humphreys K (1997) A review of the research on the effectiveness of self-help mutual aid groups. International *Journal of Psychosocial Rehabilitation* **2** 64–68.

Laub J & Sampson R (2003) *Shared Beginnings, Divergent Lives: Delinquent boys to aged 70.* Cambridge: Massachusetts: Harvard University Press: Cambridge.

McIntosh J & McKeganey N (2000) Addicts' narratives of recovery from drug use: Constructing a non-addict identity. *Social Science and Medicine* **50** 1501–1510.

Moos (2011) Processes that promote recovery from addictive disorders. In: J Kelly & W White (Eds) *Addiction Recovery Management: Theory, research and practice.* New York: Humana Press, Springer.

O'Brien C & McLellan T (1986) Myths about the treatment of addiction. *Lancet* **347** 237–240.

Putnam R (2000) *Bowling Alone: The collapse and revival of American community.* New York: Simon and Schuster.

Rethink (2008) *Getting Back to the World.* Unpublished report.

Royal Society for the Arts (2010) *Whole Person Approach: A user-centred systems approach to problem drug use.* London: RSA.

Schroeder R, Giordano P & Cernkovich S (2007) Drug use and desistance processes. *Criminology* **45** (1) 191–222.

Scott C, Foss M & Dennis M (2005) Pathways in the relapse, treatment and recovery cycle over three years. *Journal of Substance Abuse Treatment* **28** 63–72.

Teruya C & Hser Y (2010) Turning points in the life course: current findings and future research directions. *Current Drug Abuse Review* **3** (3) 189–195.

Theobold D & Farrington D (2011) Why do the crime-reducing effects of marriage vary with age? *British Journal of Criminology* **51** 136–158.

Waldorf D, Reinarman C & Murphy S (1991) *Cocaine Changes: The experience of using and quitting.* Philadelphia, PA: Temple University.

White W & Cloud W (2008) Recovery capital: a primer for addiction professionals. *Counselor* **9** (5) 22–27.

White W (2009) *Peer-Based Addiction Recovery Support: History, theory, practice, and scientific evaluation.* Chicago, IL: Great Lakes Addiction Technology Transfer Center and Philadelphia Department of Behavioural Health and Mental Retardation Services.

White W & Kurtz E (2006) The Varieties of Recovery Experience. *International Journal of Self Help and Self Care* **3** (1–2) 21–61.

Chapter 4

Recovery pathways

The Centre for Substance Abuse Treatment's (CSAT) conclusion that 58% of addicts will eventually achieve a sustained recovery from substance dependence draws upon studies using multiple methodologies, including treatment outcome research, cohort studies and general population studies (CSAT, 2009). There is relatively little information provided on who these people are or when the recovery took place, and the suspicion arises that the figure may include populations with a short duration of dependence who did not experience the same 'rock bottom' that may have characterised other recovery pathways.

This chapter sets out to explore what recovery means in terms of two sources of information and data – from studies of 'natural recovery' and from treatment outcome studies – before reviewing the evidence from recovery studies in Glasgow and Birmingham to make sense of the pathways to recovery in studies that attempted to include and incorporate a 'natural recovery' group. The aim of the chapter is to broaden the reader's analysis by separating out two populations – those whose recovery journey does not involve formal treatment services and those who recover through their own efforts, before considering the evidence from treatment outcome studies.

What is 'natural recovery'?

Robins (1973) studied the patterns of drug use in US soldiers returning from Vietnam. A sample of 898 men who returned from Vietnam in 1971 was interviewed the following year, ranging from eight to 12 months after their return. Approximately 20% of the enlisted men were dependent on heroin while in Vietnam. Upon return, only 10% of those addicted in Vietnam reported using heroin or other opiates between the time of their return and the interview, and only one per cent became re-addicted. At the time of the interview, only two per cent (eight per cent of those who were dependent users in Vietnam) reported continued drug use. Veterans did equally well regardless of whether they sought addiction treatment on their return or not. What is more, those who continued use after returning to the US were typically those who had initiated drug use before going to Vietnam.

One of the main conclusions that can be drawn from Robins' work is that substance use is strongly linked to the context of use – the environment, choices and social mores in operation at the time of initial and of ongoing use, and that if those conditions are shifted, continuation of use cannot be explained simply in terms of 'habituation' or 'dependence'. A second major conclusion from the study is that some people simply stop using without recourse to specialist treatment interventions such as detoxification regimes or psychological therapies. Such a resolution has been referred to as 'natural recovery' or 'auto-remission' and has been evidenced in a number of US and European studies (for example, Winick, 1962; Scharse, 1966; Robins, 1973; O'Donnell *et al,* 1976; Klingemann, 1991; Cunningham, 2000).

The earliest evidence of natural recovery came from Winick's *Maturing Out of Narcotic Addiction* study (1962). Winick examined records kept by the Federal Bureau of Narcotics and found that as addicts approached 35–40 years they tended to 'drop out' of the files, which suggested that they had experienced a transformational life process, similar to those affecting adolescents 'maturing out' of juvenile delinquency. The findings of this study have been subsequently contested on the grounds that the data sources (primarily criminal justice system engagement) are insufficient evidence of recovery, and so Winick's model has been criticised for providing too optimistic a model of desistance.

More typically, the evidence comes from either population surveys or from in-depth research interviews with samples responding to advertisements. As individuals who have successfully stopped without accessing treatment are more elusive, different research methods are required and it is very difficult to quantify how often this happens. Additionally, researchers will have to rely on retrospective accounts of those who believe that they have recovered (and indeed that they were formerly dependent), generating scepticism in some professionals about whether they were ever 'really' addicted or indeed that they have 'actually' recovered.

Using population data, Sobell *et al* (1996) reported rates of 75% and 77% recovery without formal help in drinkers in remission. Cunningham (2000) assessed recovery from a range of substances and reported that the use of any formal treatment ranged from 43.1% for cannabis to 90.7% for heroin, with 59.7% of cocaine users seeking formal treatment at some point in their recovery journey. Thus, where general population surveys methods are used, it becomes apparent that the most common method of achieving recovery does not involve accessing formal treatment and will be achieved through self-selected methods. The increased availability of self-help guides and online resources may suggest that such approaches increase in prevalence and may further blur the distinction between treated and natural forms of recovery.

More of the work on natural recovery comes from in-depth social research. Klingemann's (1991) study of 30 former dependent drinkers and 30 formerly heroin-dependent users in Switzerland developed a typology of motivation to stop in a 'auto-remission' group. One group of people in recovery was described as 'hitting bottom', for example, experiencing physical, interpersonal, and psychological collapse. Within this group, one sub-sample was characterised by Klingemann as 'cross-road types', who act on the basis of a single crisis (such as health or psychological problems); and another sub-sample consisted of 'pressure-sensitive types', who reacted positively to social pressure which forced them to choose between a life of conformity or addiction. A third group was described as having had esoteric or religious experiences as turning points. So, within the natural recovery population at least, the idea that individuals have to hit some kind of 'rock bottom' does not appear to be sustained.

However, the most widely cited study of natural recovery was carried out by Granfield and Cloud (2001) in a study that involved semi-structured interviews with 46 former drug or alcohol-dependent persons who had recovered without treatment. Granfield and Cloud (2001) reported that the respondents in the study discounted the use of self-help groups because they saw themselves as 'efficacious people' who often prided themselves on past accomplishments. The study added to the social context model of recovery by noting that many participants had a great deal to lose if they continued their substance abuse. They noted that the subjects in their study *'had jobs, supportive families, high school and college credentials, and other social supports that gave them reasons to alter their drug-taking behaviour,'* and added that *'having much to lose'* gave their respondents *'incentives to transform their lives'* (Granfield & Cloud, 2001, p55).

In a study of cocaine users, Waldorf *et al* (1991) found that many participants who had supportive elements in their lives (a job, family, and other close emotional supports) were able to 'walk away' from very heavy cocaine use. Waldorf *et al* (1991) suggested that the 'social context' of drug users' lives might positively influence their ability to discontinue drug use. The key conclusions from natural recovery studies are that existing resources and binds to conventional society may well provide some form of 'escape clause' from substance problems, but also suggest the diversity of routes out of addiction that do not involve mutual aid groups or through formal treatment services. This form of research also emphasises both choice and self-determination as key components of recovery, linked to the utilisation of personal and social resources, akin to the recovery capital model proposed in Chapter 3. This is consistent with White's (1996) assertion that the transition from addiction to recovery is often a journey from one culture to another, each with its own distinct language, values and rituals.

Recovery and treatment

While there is a small number of natural recovery studies, they are primarily American and use methodologies (typically based on population surveys or opportunistic recruitment) that may be less likely to access the most problematic and entrenched substance users. For this reason, it is important to give some attention to recovery via formal treatment services, with the primary method of research being observational research studies.

One of the earliest longitudinal cohort studies was conducted in the US by Vaillant, who recruited 100 New York City male addicts admitted to Lexington Hospital in 1952 and 1953 (Vaillant, 1973). The majority of the sample was found to have relapsed after leaving Lexington, but drug use trends over time were towards reduced opiate use. Vaillant found that 22% were abstinent at the five-year follow-up point, and 37% at the 10-year point.

The next major American treatment outcome study was the Drug Abuse Reporting Programme (DARP) (Simpson & Sells, 1990). In DARP, 53% of patients who had been daily users of opioids before treatment were not daily opioid users at one year after the baseline interview, and continued improvement was observed over time until year six when the proportion of non-users stabilised at 58% for 'any' use and 75% for 'daily' use. At the time of the 12-year follow-up the favourable outcome was retained, with the proportion of non-users slightly increasing to 61% and 76% for 'any' use and for 'daily' use respectively (Simpson & Sells, 1990).

In 1995, the National Treatment Outcome Research Study (NTORS) recruited 1,075 patients from 54 treatment programmes using a design similar to the US treatment outcome studies (National Addiction Centre, 2001). Four treatment modalities were included in the study – methadone reduction, methadone maintenance, inpatient detoxification and residential rehabilitation. One year after intake to treatment, outcome data was obtained for 769 patients (72%) and subsequent follow-ups at two and four to five years were conducted with a random, stratified sample of patients. At one year follow-up, within the residential settings, the percentage of clients from the rehabilitation programmes who were abstinent from illicit opiates increased from 27% at intake to 58% at one year follow-up; while the proportion of regular users fell from 63% to 33% (Gossop *et al,* 1998). Gossop *et al* (2002), who reported on the two-year outcomes from the NTORS, found that 48% of admissions to residential treatment were abstinent from all opiates, with the majority of this group sustaining abstinence over the full four to five year follow-up period and high rates of continuity of abstinence.

The follow-up to the NTORS was the Drug Treatment Outcomes Research Study (DTORS) (Home Office, 2009), which used a 12-month window to assess treatment outcomes, supplemented by a qualitative assessment of 'treatment-related issues' and a cost effectiveness analysis. In this study, 1,796 drug users were recruited from 342 agencies, of whom 1,131 were followed up three to five months later and 504 11–13 months after the baseline assessment. The main conclusions were that DTORS outcomes were equivalent or more positive for treatment effectiveness than those found in NTORS (National Addiction Centre, 2001). Employment rates increased from nine per cent at baseline to 11% at follow-up one and 16% at follow-up two – however, the proportion of participants classed as unable to work also increased over the course of the study follow-ups. Similarly, offending reduced from a self-reported level of 40% at baseline to 21% at first follow-up and 16% at second follow-up. Among heroin users involved in the baseline interviews, 44% had stopped using at first follow-up and 49% at second follow-up, and there were consistent reductions in all of the other major substances assessed over the course of the follow-up periods. However, the high drop-out rate in the DTORS study makes these conclusions tentative.

In Scotland, the Scottish Drug Treatment Outcome Research Study (DORIS) (McKeganey *et al,* 2006) recruited 1,007 drug misusers from 33 agencies, including five prisons. The study involved follow-up assessments at eight months, 16 months and 33 months post-intake to the study, achieving a 70% follow-up rate at the 33-month follow-up point. While there are initial improvements to eight months, these taper off at the subsequent follow-up points. The authors concluded that, compared to other community programmes, residential rehabilitation clients were twice as likely to be abstinent at 33 months, and while methadone maintenance treatment was associated with reductions in heroin use it was not successful in promoting abstinence. The authors also asked treatment clients what they wanted from services, with long-term abstinence and recovery cited much more frequently than substitute prescribing or harm-reduction goals. In a paper drawn from the study, McKeganey *et al* (2006) reported on 695 follow-ups at 33 months and found that only 5.9% of females and 9.0% of males were abstinent in the 90 days prior to interview. The DORIS study was particularly contentious as the authors set great store by abstinence rates, and were extremely critical of the perceived failure of maintenance prescribing to enable clients to achieve significant changes in working and social engagement.

In a secondary analysis of the DORIS data examining the uptake of employment during the period of the study, McIntosh *et al* (2008) reported that 20.1% of the follow-up sample (140/695) had been in paid employment since the previous interview. The main predictors of achieving employment were being younger, having lower levels of crime involvement, and receiving support from the treatment agency with training and education or with obtaining a job. Treatment modality was not linked to employment status, suggesting that maintenance treatments are not incompatible with meaningful engagement but also that the overall rates of work are relatively low.

What are the key conclusions from the treatment research literature?

The first thing that makes generalisation problematic is that the measures used, the treatment centre types studied and the follow-up points have differed from one study to another. There are also cohort and national differences that add complications. Nonetheless, there are grounds for supporting the basic 'treatment works' mantra, although these grounds relate much more to impact on criminality, risk and health than they do to long-term desistance and change. So the conclusion that treatment works is

Addiction Recovery: A movement for social change and personal growth in the UK ©
Pavilion Publishing (Brighton) Ltd 2012

followed by a caution that these studies have rarely been conducted from a recovery perspective and so the ambitious goals of increasing hope, well-being and belonging have not been measured satisfactorily, nor have the issues of supportive networks or meaningful activities been addressed sufficiently.

Recent recovery research in the UK

Over the course of the last 10 years, Best and colleagues have conducted a series of research studies collecting recovery stories from different parts of the UK using a range of research methods. Around 1,000 recovery stories have been collected as part of this endeavour, and this number is increasing as the research effort continues. In total, four of these studies will be summarised and an overall review will be presented.

The first of these investigations was an opportunistic study using a brief self-completion questionnaire that tapped into the fact that a substantial proportion of drug workers, particularly those in non-statutory treatment services, were themselves in recovery (Best *et al*, 2008). It was based on the accounts of 107 former heroin users who were predominantly working in the addictions field at the time of the survey. On average, participants had heroin careers lasting for just under 10 years, punctuated by an average of 2.6 treatment episodes and 3.1 periods of abstinence. When asked what enabled them to finally give up using heroin, the answer was most commonly about 'having had enough' – a gradual process of not wanting to live that life any more, but also involving an event – family or health-related in many cases, that finally gave them the impetus to make the initial change. However, the key finding from this study was that participants readily differentiated between the factors that allowed them to achieve abstinence and the factors that allowed them to sustain it. The most important factors in sustaining recovery were social network factors (moving away from drug-using friends and support from non-using friends) and practical factors (accommodation and employment) as well as religious or spiritual factors. However, this was a limited sample and so a series of further studies were undertaken in Birmingham and Glasgow.

In a study of former drinkers accessed through aftercare services and recovery community groups in Birmingham, Hibbert and Best (2011) recruited 53 former alcoholics who were either one to five years or more than five years since their last alcoholic drink. The primary aim was to assess whether quality of life continued to grow with increasing time in recovery. However, using the World Health Organization's (WHO) measure of quality of life, the study also showed that those with longer recovery actually reported significantly higher quality of life satisfaction with both their social networks and with their engagement in their local neighbourhoods than people who had never been addicted. This phenomenon – known as being 'better than well' – suggests that those who do come out the other end of addiction will often come out as stronger and better people. This is a fundamental challenge to the idea that 'getting better' is a process of shedding symptoms and pathologies and instead suggests that recovery is a process of growth and well-being that will not only exceed pre-morbid states of functioning but will also surpass that of people who have never been through the same 're-birth' and change process. It is also consistent with the idea that recovery is an ongoing process and journey with those who achieve lengthy periods of sobriety and active recovery providing a core of 'champions' from whom others can garner hope and inspiration, as well as direct learning of the techniques and methods of recovery.

In the Glasgow recovery study, Best *et al* (2011, in press) attempted to take this analysis of quality of life further. Consistent with the sample of Birmingham drinkers, from a study of 205 people who described themselves as in recovery from either heroin (98) or alcohol (107), a main finding was that the longer the time since the last use of alcohol or heroin was associated with a significantly better quality of life at the time of interview. However, two new predictors of recovery were also identified. One of the key findings reported was the prominent role played by engagement in meaningful activities. Not only was this associated with better day-to-day functioning (eg. less anxiety and depression; fewer physical health symptoms; as well as better self-esteem and self-efficacy), it was also the single most powerful predictor of overall quality of life in the study. Those who were engaged in daily activities – working, training, volunteering, group participation and parenting – were happier and functioned better than those not engaged in such activities. The second most powerful predictor of quality of life was the number of people in recovery social networks – in other words, being active and having a support network of people in recovery were very powerful predictors of life quality among those in recovery.

There are also other important lessons from this work – the first being that it was not difficult to find people who described themselves as being in recovery. While issues persist about there being hidden populations of people in recovery, most participants in the studies were very pleased to tell their

Addiction Recovery: A movement for social change and personal growth in the UK © Pavilion Publishing (Brighton) Ltd 2012

stories and to be asked to do so and, even among those whose anonymity was protected by involvement in 12-step fellowships, there was a willingness to help recruit among friends and peers. While questions of sampling are problematic in research terms, there are key questions that can be addressed about salience and visibility of recovery groups and communities.

The other major findings are about what recovery looks like – it is a process of growth that is socially mediated and linked to engagement and activity.

The recovery story so far

There are two important conclusions to draw from the studies of natural recovery. The first is that recovery will frequently involve no contact with specialist treatment services and that the experiences of those who do recover in this way often involve movement and attraction towards other groups and activities that result in and result from changes in perceived identity. Within specialist treatment settings there is evidence that a sizeable group of presenters will achieve lasting abstinence but that the type of service engaged with may influence that outcome. It is also difficult to judge treatment outcome studies in recovery terms as that has rarely been their goal and so there has been a disproportionate focus on changes in substance use as the sole marker of recovery. Finally, the author's own early work on recovery would suggest that recovery populations are accessible to researchers, but that this requires a shift in methods and research rationale but that the populations of people in recovery who can be found will typically be very positive about telling their own story. And those stories, while diverse and intensely personal, share some common characteristics – recovery is a journey that for most people is ongoing; it is a journey that involves 'transcendence' of problems; recovery will generally be based around shifts in social networks that generate a sense of purpose, a sense of belonging and a belief that recovery is transformative.

Key learning points

■ Treatment is not always required for recovery and there is a body of international research that has described a 'natural recovery'.

■ Although addiction is a chronic, relapsing condition and people are never 'safe' from relapse, there is good evidence that a substantial proportion of those who access abstinence-based treatment will achieve and sustain their recovery.

- If the majority of treatment is based on indefinite substitution treatments, then the rates of abstinent recovery are likely to be reduced and individuals' addiction careers prolonged.

- Where UK studies of recovery have been undertaken, they show easily accessible communities of recovery, many of whom will have been aided in their recovery journeys by mutual aid groups.

- Recovery does not stop with symptom-reduction. Research in Birmingham supports the idea that people can be 'better than well' and continue to grow in their sense of well-being and positive quality of life.

References

Best D, Ghufran S, Day E, Ray R & Loaring J (2008) Breaking the habit: a retrospective analysis of desistance factors among formerly problematic heroin users. *Drug and Alcohol Review* **27** (6) 619–624.

Best D, Gow J, Knox T, Taylor A, Groshkova T & White W (2011, in press) Mapping the recovery stories of drinkers and drug users in Glasgow: quality of life and its predictors. *Journal of Drug Issues*.

Centre for Substance Abuse Treatment (2009) *Guiding Principles and Elements of Recovery-Oriented Systems of Care: What do we know from the research?* Rockville, MD: Centre for Substance Abuse Treatment.

Cunningham J (2000) Remissions from drug dependence: is treatment a prerequisite? *Drug and Alcohol Dependence* **59** (3) 211–213.

Gossop M, Marsden J, Stewart D, Lehman P, Wilson A & Segar G (1998) Substance use, health and social problems of service users at 54 drug treatment agencies. Intake data from the National Treatment Outcome Research Study. *British Journal of Psychiatry* **173** 166 –171.

Gossop M, Stewart D, Treacy S & Marsden J (2002) A prospective study of mortality among drug misusers during a 4-year period after seeking treatment. *Addiction* **97** 39–47.

Granfield R & Cloud W (2001) Social context and 'natural recovery': the role of social capital in the resolution of drug-associated problems. *Substance Use and Misuse* **36** 1543–1570.

Hibbert L & Best D (2011) Assessing recovery and functioning in former problem drinkers at different stages of their recovery journey. *Drug and Alcohol Review* **30** 12–20.

Home Office (2009) *The Drug Treatment Outcomes Research Study (DTORS): Final outcomes report (3rd edition)*. Available at: http://rds.homeoffice.gov.uk/rds/pdfs09/horr24c.pdf (accessed October 2011).

Klingemann H (1991) The motivation for change from problem alcohol and heroin use. *British Journal of Addiction* **86** 727–744.

McKeganey NP, Bloor MJ, Robertson M, Neale J & McDougall J (2006) Abstinence and drug abuse treatment: Results from the Drug Outcome Research in Scotland Study. *Drugs: Education, Prevention and Policy* **13** (6) 537–550.

McIntosh J, Bloor MJ & Robertson M (2008) The health benefits of reductions in individuals' use of illegal drugs. *Journal of Substance Use* **13** (4) 247–254.

National Addiction Centre (2001) *NTORS After Five Years: The National Treatment Outcome Research study.* London: Crown Copyright.

O'Donnell J, Voss H & Clayton R (1976) *Young Men and Drugs: A nationwide survey.* Washington: National Institute on Drug Abuse.

Robins LN (1973) *The Vietnam Drug User Returns.* Washington DC: US Government Printing Office.

Scharse R (1966) Cessation patterns among neophyte heroin users. *International Journal of Addictions* **1** (2) 23–32.

Simpson DD & Sells SB (Eds) (1990) *Opioid Addiction and Treatment: A 12-year follow-up.* Malabar, FL: Robert E. Krieger Publishing Company.

Sobell LC, Cunningham JA & Sobell MB (1996) Recovery from alcohol problems with and without treatment: prevalence in two population surveys. *American Journal of Public Health* **86** (7) 966–972.

Vaillant GE (1973) A 20 year follow-up of New York narcotic addicts. *Archives of General Psychiatry* **29** 237–241.

Waldorf D, Reinarman C & Murphy S (1991) *Cocaine Changes: The experience of using and quitting.* Philadelphia, PA: Temple University.

White W (1996) *Pathways from the Culture of Addiction to the Culture of Recovery.* Center City, MN: Hazelden.

Winick C (1962) *Maturing Out of Narcotics Addiction.* New York: United Nations Office on Drugs and Crime.

Chapter 5

Recovery and treatment

This chapter builds on the discussion in Chapter 4 by switching focus to the relationship between specialist UK drug treatment as it is typically delivered and the transition to a recovery focus. The primary concern will be opiate substitution treatment, particularly methadone treatment, as it is experienced by clients accessing specialist services. The focus will then switch to other forms of treatment – inpatient detoxification and both residential and community rehabilitation – in an attempt to understand the role of specialist intervention in enabling and supporting long-term recovery and change.

What is the client experience of the treatment process?

As preparation for the implementation of a treatment effectiveness model (discussed later in this chapter), Best and colleagues repeated a city-wide audit of structured drug treatment that included both standard and criminal justice treatments. This work was largely based on workers' accounts of their contact with clients on their clinical caseload and has been published in two academic papers (Best *et al,* 2009a; Best *et al,* 2009b). Effectively, the audit and the resulting papers attempted to assess what treatment means for the average client in drug services in a large city – in this case, Birmingham. The results were not encouraging – most clients were due to be seen between once a fortnight and once a month, and they were typically seen by their worker for an average time of 45 minutes. Of that 45 minutes, around half was taken up with 'case management' activities such as management of the methadone prescription, completion of assessment and review documentation, drug testing and reviewing the results, with only around 10 minutes on average spent on anything that could be characterised as a psychological or psychosocial intervention. Also, attendance rates were typically only around 50%, so in practice the amount of contact time with workers was around 45 minutes per month and psychosocial interventions of only 10 minutes per month, or two hours per year. Thus, the question of whether treatment is good enough is superseded by the much more urgent question of why the typical client receives so little of it.

This study has been widely criticised for taking a very narrow view of 'therapeutic interventions' and for attacking an outmoded and atypical delivery of treatment. However, more recently, Wisely (2010) used a similar approach to assess what treatment meant for clients in services in Salford. Wisely reported that more than half of the clients interviewed (29 out of 55) had seen their worker for 20 minutes or less at the last 'treatment session' and with only 11% reporting that their employment status and 22% their education status had changed since completing treatment. This suggests that many drug users accessing primarily opiate substitution treatments only receive a 'script and a chat', which bears little resemblance to the evidence-based psychological interventions that the empirical rationale for maintenance prescribing is based on.

However, this minimal form of intervention affects not only the clients who receive it but also the workers who are involved in the management of these transactional treatment relationships. In a study of Dutch methadone programmes, Loth *et al* (2007) described an overall effect where methadone treatment had initially been successful, but that this had deteriorated in subsequent years. At the time of writing, around 13,000 people were receiving methadone on a daily dispensing basis in one of 85 specialist clinics in the Netherlands. Loth *et al* (2007) argued that treatment quality had deteriorated because of the high number of patients to be treated within an hour, high staff turnover, incidents of aggression at the clinics and the limited facilities available. When interviewing staff, the authors concluded that staff often had *'a feeling of shame about their attitudes towards patients. For example, the short contacts were filled with computer activities and not with patient-directed conversations'* (Loth *et al*, 2007, p428). Staff members were often disenfranchised and alienated and regarded little of their work as being therapeutic; this then had an impact on their clients.

In northwest England, Honor and Karpusheff (2010) conducted a baseline review of treatment experiences among problem drug users. As reported above, those engaged in methadone substitution treatment were seen infrequently (74% were seen fortnightly or less) and for short periods of time (64% for 15 minutes or less) – in total, the authors concluded that people see their worker for 21 minutes every 2.7 weeks. Honor and Karpusheff conclude that *'many people enter treatment, but their experiences of treatment services do not always meet their expectations; they may even limit them'* (Honor & Karpusheff, 2010, p97). This is the most recent in a series of local assessments of drug-using populations in and out of treatment that suggest treatment can offer some quick benefits to people but is rarely characterised as a means for achieving long-term abstinence. One of the major challenges for the treatment system is that it does not prolong addiction careers unnecessarily and that it does not persist as an alternative to recovery.

How has this situation arisen? In England, the establishment of targets around numbers in treatment has led to opiate substitution treatment, generally in the form of methadone prescribing, becoming the default intervention not only for clients who self-refer into treatment but also those caught in the net of quasi-coercion through the criminal justice system, through a range of early interventions and alternative community disposals. For many of those who end up in structured drug treatment, what this means is that they receive a prescription and little else. The next section of this chapter will attempt to demonstrate that there is a supportive evidence base for methadone maintenance treatment but not one that is delivered in practice in most locations in the UK.

The rationale and evidence for methadone treatment

Prendergast *et al* (2002) conducted a meta-analysis of 78 studies conducted between 1965 and 1996 comparing no or minimal treatment with evidence-based drug treatments. The authors concluded that treatment is effective in both reducing substance use and in reducing crime, and providing an empirical justification for the claim that 'treatment works' – something that seems to be borne out in the review of treatment outcome studies in Chapter 4.

In a Cochrane review, Amato *et al* (2008) found considerable supporting evidence for methadone treatment based on the effective combined delivery of treatment with psychosocial interventions. From its inception, the rationale of effective opiate substitution treatment has been a combination of prescription plus 'wraparound services' plus psychosocial interventions. The problem, however, is delivery. As Newman (1976) argued, as early as the 1970s, in a paper entitled *Methadone Maintenance: It ain't what it used to be*, he concludes that the aim of reintegrating patients into society has not been a success and that *'the painful and inescapable reality is that the failure lies with those of us who operate methadone programmes and who also share the belief that while our patients might be slightly healthier and less likely to commit crimes, they remain junkies'* (Newman, 1976, p185).

This is the evidence base that prompted a group of international experts to proclaim: *'the media repeatedly report a view of methadone treatment that is simply contrary to the extensively documented worldwide clinical and research experience of many decades. Reliable and persistent research shows that methadone treatment substantially reduces death, crime, HIV infection and drug use while also assisting social functioning such as improved education, training, parenting and employment'* (Robertson, Bird, Bruce, Budd, Carrieri, Christie, Cockayne, Kastelic, Fischer, Gourlay, Griffin, Reisinger, Kamarulzaman, Lee, McGovern, Macleod, Kerr, Nelles, Newman, Malinowska-Sempruch, Torrners, Drucker, Hickman, Jay, Jospeh, Parrino, Meyer-Thopson, Ford & Strang, 2010). The reason for listing such a telephone directory of eminent names is to make clear, as the signatories did, that methadone treatment is viewed in clinical academic circles as non-contentious and evidence-based.

What are the grounds for concern?

The first concern is who gets methadone. In one of the most well-established recovery outcome studies, reviewed by Skipper and Dupont in 2011, five-year abstinence rates of 79% were achieved and return to work rates of 96% in a cohort of alcohol and drug problem-using physicians. The programme was the Physician Health Programs (PHP), and with such outcomes it provides an insight into the core elements of a successful intervention. Among the 'key ingredients' identified by the authors were: identifying a motivational fulcrum; comprehensive assessment and treatment; a care management oversight role; high expectations of abstinence; assertive linkage to recovery support groups; sustained monitoring and where necessary re-intervention; re-interventions taking place at a higher level of intensity; and the above elements integrated within a comprehensive programme. Of the 904 people evaluated on the programme, more than 300 were primary opiate users (over half of whom used intravenously). Yet, the authors note that *'only one participant of the 904 was placed on methadone and that participant was not practicing medicine at the time of the study'* (Skipper & Dupont, 2011, p293)

There is a reason why such a powerful recovery study does not include widespread use of *'the extensively documented worldwide clinical and research experience of many decades'* (Robertson *et al*, 2010). There are some problems in comparing the treatments received by doctors in recovery with the 'typical' client population, who will have significantly fewer social capital resources. Pronouncements about evidence-based treatments combined with an unwillingness to use it with a doctor population suggest that methadone is a good treatment for reducing crime and injecting risk, but that it has a reduced likelihood (although not impossibility) of adequate social engagement and participation.

Where does this mismatch occur? One area is around the possible effects of methadone on cognitive functioning. Mintzer *et al* (2005) report that methadone clients showed markedly greater deficits than both a control group and an abstinent group in four areas of executive function – short-term memory, attention, decision-making and planning. In applying this to a UK treatment population, King and Best (2010) found average verbal IQ scores of 77 in a group of methadone maintained patients, while the same patients showed almost no deficit in their performance IQ. While this study was cross-sectional, and so deficits may have pre-dated the prescription of methadone, it is telling that the strongest correlate of low verbal IQ was high methadone dose. There is a significant concern that methadone may be associated with a suppression of cognitive functioning that is not compatible with the long-term planning for recovery and change, or with the effective engagement in social groups and family activities, for a substantial proportion of clients.

There is also a long history of concerns that the lifestyle associated with methadone maintenance is problematic. Preble and Casey (1969) introduced the idea of 'methadone, wine and welfare' in connection with the idea that, for a substantial proportion of clients, methadone prescription is associated with a lifestyle of heavy drinking, low levels of employment and low motivation to change. Best *et al*'s (1998) work in London suggests that long-term methadone prescribing is associated with a significant risk of problem drinking, poor diet and sleep patterns, and an ongoing use of a range of prescribed, diverted and illicit drugs. Recent studies have also suggested possible adverse effects on bone density, but the primary problem is the difficulty of stagnation.

Thus, the fundamental criticism of the methadone maintenance model, at least as it is applied in the UK in many specialist teams, is that it looks much more like palliative care than drug treatment. While there is a strong evidence base, that evidence base generally relates to public health and public safety and does not pay sufficient attention to the risk of iatrogenic effects for clients who may experience initial gains in life quality and stability, which then dissipate rapidly into stasis and stagnation. This effect is experienced in clinical teams who, beset by large caseloads and limited time, exchange a therapeutic model for a case management one that is overwhelmed by concerns about the prescription and its safe management. Thus, the problem is not primarily about methadone and its effectiveness but about its utilisation in a sub-therapeutic model that does not generate the hope, belief or expectation that recovery is possible.

Treatment effectiveness

The concern about treatment effectiveness is not a uniquely UK phenomenon. In the US, McLellan (2006) bemoaned the lack of consistent implementation of evidence-based interventions in routine addiction treatment practice and suggests that this has its origins in group-based service delivery and the high rates of turnover in generally poorly qualified staff. In the UK, this problem is less apparent in an area where the primary mechanism of client engagement is one-to-one work and there are high levels of trained and qualified staff. Nonetheless, as documented above, problems exist in delivering evidence-based psychological or psychosocial interventions in the UK – while NICE has provided technology appraisals of effective interventions, these are rarely applied in practice. This is the issue of 'technology transfer' – how to translate research trial evidence to the everyday context of clinical engagement.

This work has been led by Professor Dwayne Simpson and his team at the Institute of Behavioural Research at Texas Christian University and has been summarised in a paper on the Treatment Process Model (Simpson, 2004). In this model, Simpson outlines a model for change based on three clear stages:

- motivation and engagement
- psychosocial change
- recovery and reintegration.

Addiction Recovery: A movement for social change and personal growth in the UK ©
Pavilion Publishing (Brighton) Ltd 2012

In this model, the first phase of therapeutic contact has two clear objectives – developing a therapeutic relationship and motivating the client to change (and generating the aspiration and belief that change and recovery are possible). The model rests on the idea that meaningful change in treatment is reliant on a strong therapeutic bond between the client and the worker and only once this is established is it meaningful to work towards changes in attitudes and behaviours. Those initial changes are then supported by a series of targeted interventions that are linked to social reintegration, including a focus on communications, on families and relationships, and on engagement with mutual aid recovery groups.

The overall model of therapeutic change is implemented through a series of brief manualised interventions (originally intended to be delivered over four to six sessions in either individual or group settings). These are based on a technique called Node Link Mapping that is based on shared working to improve the quality of communication, client empowerment and ownership of the therapeutic process, and so the quality of the therapeutic alliance. In the UK, this approach was implemented in two pilot projects – the International Treatment Effectiveness Project and the Birmingham Treatment Effectiveness Initiative (BTEI) and is now widely used across the UK. The papers deriving from these initiatives show there is a strong relationship between workers' experiences and attitudes and the quality of the therapeutic relationship (Simpson *et al*, 2009; Best *et al,* 2009c). In a study that linked assessment of workers' beliefs about organisational functioning and their own efficacy and influence with clients' ratings of treatment engagement there were consistent positive associations reported.

In other words, as Simpson *et al* (2009) previously showed in the US, where workers were positive about their working environments, and had positive beliefs about their own capacity to enable client recovery, clients reported more satisfaction with treatment, more positive therapeutic relationships and more active participation in treatment. From a recovery perspective, this series of studies is crucial as it suggests a central role for drug workers in supporting and enabling the change process.

What is the role of treatment and keyworking in a recovery model?

Contrary to the belief that recovery is an 'anti-treatment' agenda, there is a crucial role for treatment services, and particularly for drug workers, in supporting and enabling recovery. As outlined in Chapter 3, there are fundamental clinical prerequisites for many people with addiction problems – physical sequelae of their substance use (including blood-borne viruses, injecting site injuries and management of physical dependence), psychological and psychiatric problems that need to be assessed and treated where appropriate, and basic advice and guidance to be given, including support in reducing the harms around their substance use. So this 'acute' phase of intervention is by no means diminished within a recovery model, and there may also come a time when people will need specialist interventions around agonist (eg. buprenorphine) and antagonist (eg. naltrexone) prescribing and for detoxification.

In *Pathways from the Culture of Addiction to the Culture of Recovery,* White (1990) outlines six key tasks for the key worker in enabling and supporting the recovery process.

1. Creating awareness of the excessive behaviour.
2. Teaching the client that excess is a developmental stage in the recovery journey.
3. Encouraging daily rituals for self-assessment and focus.
4. Teaching sobriety-based coping skills.
5. Facilitating the establishment of a sobriety-based social network.
6. Periodic re-assessment to manage the risk of relapse.

However, the role of the key worker or counsellor is fundamentally different in a recovery model, as is the nature of the relationship. There are primarily three roles that are played by workers in supporting and enabling a recovery journey.

1. Inspiration and motivation.
2. Bridging and guiding.
3. Transmission of specialist knowledge.

Addiction Recovery: A movement for social change and personal growth in the UK ©
Pavilion Publishing (Brighton) Ltd 2012

Within a developmental model, and entirely consistent with the Treatment Process Model (Simpson, 2004), the role of the worker is to be a 'turning point' in the addiction career. In many of the narratives of recovery that have formed the basis for this book, it is specific individuals who have led drug and alcohol addicts to believe that change is possible. To do this, there has to be a real personal bond that develops between the worker and the client – a 'spark' – that is the basis for nurturing the belief that recovery is possible, that a partnership between the two can start that journey and that the relationship can be a core form of social capital from which personal growth can blossom. Within a recovery model, the crucial aspect of the therapeutic relationship is not to do with evidence-based interventions or professional skills, but an intimate human relationship that can regenerate or inspire hope and belief. In developmental terms, it is the intensity and power of the relationship that enables it to be a tipping point.

The second role is that of bridging and guiding. The core conclusion from the service delivery analysis carried out by Best *et al* (2009a; 2009b) is that, irrespective of whether treatment is good enough, for the vast majority of people it is not enough. To be seen for 45 minutes once every fortnight is unlikely to be a turning point unless it is supported and sustained by changes in social groups and networks, and by what people do for the ensuing two weeks. To that extent, one of the fundamental shifts in a recovery model is that workers cannot passively sit behind desks, waiting for client appointment times, to dispense evidence-based interventions, vouchers, prescriptions and wisdom between four and eight times a day. They have to be the 'assertive linkage' facilitator that introduces their clients to inspirational figures in the recovery community, to safe and supportive groups of recovering addicts, to pathways to interests, hobbies, education and training, and to the other key professionals who may also inspire and motivate and support. Thus, the model for work must change from that of 'expert' dislocated within a specialist therapeutic location to 'partner' guiding and leading, and actively engaging with community supports and resources to enable and support change.

And finally there is a clear role for the delivery of evidence-based psychosocial interventions, as promoted by the National Institute of Health and Clinical Excellence (NICE, 2007), but it is deliberately the last thing to be listed here. For most clients in the UK, seen only in 30–45 minutes slots at infrequent intervals, where much of the time is required to be spent on the completion of paperwork, on management of prescriptions and on other administrative tasks, there is limited opportunity for doing more than simple mapping activities that can build into therapeutic binding activities and simple techniques for enabling the growth of social capital. The Node Link Mapping work suggests that much of this activity could and should be done by peers in non-specialist settings.

Overview and conclusions

The purpose of this chapter has not been to talk about treatment in an abstract sense but as it is typically received by drug users in the UK – where for the majority of people this means a brief and infrequent session with a worker and a prescription – most likely to be of methadone – on an ongoing basis. The configuration of treatment services is a barrier to the delivery of not only evidence-based psychosocial interventions but also to the embedding of 'treatment' within their own communities as an asset that can contribute to the development of supportive recovery networks. Within the developmental recovery model, workers and services can be crucial agents of change, but primarily through inter-personal relationships and by guiding people to supportive groups and inspiring individuals. For this to happen, most specialist treatment services will need to change from islands of clinical expertise to active participants in local communities whose tasks are as much interpersonal as they are 'professional'. One of the things that a recovery philosophy demands is a change in relationships between clients and workers (whatever labels are used here) from expert–patient to partnership. This is a massive challenge to workers whose privileged status should not be threatened by a move to closer and more equitable relationships with clients, and this will be a huge barrier to overcome.

Key learning points

- There is nothing incompatible about recovery and treatment, and one of the big challenges in the UK is to overcome the suggestion that they are alternatives.

- In part, this results from the dominance of a harm reduction model that is based on methadone prescribing with little adjunct treatment that has focused on public health and public safety outcomes at the expense of personal choice and well-being.

■ Treatment needs to be based on active engagement with local communities and the most important recovery focus that specialist treatment can offer is links to those who can convey hope and belief that recovery is possible.

■ Workers can be a key catalyst in inspiring hope for recovery and a key bridge in linking people to those further down the road of recovery.

■ Specialist treatment services cannot exist in isolation and they must be a part of the communities their clients come from and become an active asset in the development of recovery communities.

References

Amato L, Minozzi S, Davoli M, Vecchi S, Ferri M & Mayet S (2008) Psychosocial combined with agonist maintenance treatments versus agonist maintenance treatments alone for treatment of opioid dependence. *Cochrane Database of Systematic Reviews* **4** CD004147.

Best D, Lehmann P, Gossop M, Harris J, Noble J & Strang J (1998) Eating too little, smoking and drinking too much: wider lifestyle problems among methadone maintenance patients. *Addiction Research* **6** (6) 489–498.

Best D, Day E, Morgan B, Oza T, Copello A & Gossop M (2009a) What treatment means in practice: An analysis of the therapeutic activity provided in criminal justice drug treatment services in Birmingham, England. *Addiction Research and Theory* **17** (6) 678–687.

Best D, Wood K, Sweeting R, Morgan B & Day E (2009b) Fitting a quart into a black box: Keyworking in quasi-coercive drug treatment in England. *Drugs: Education, Prevention and Policy* **16** (6) 1–18.

Best D, Day E, Campbell A, Simpson D & Flynn P (2009c) Relationship between drug treatment engagement and criminal thinking style among drug-using offenders. *European Addiction Research* **15** 71–77.

Honor S & Karpusheff J (2010) *More Than This: Problem drug use across Cumbria.* Unpublished report.

King R & Best D (2010) Cognitive functioning and cognitive style among drug users in maintenance substitution treatment. *Drugs: Education, Prevention and Policy* **18** (2) 1–8.

Loth C, Schippers G, Hart H & van de Wijngaart G (2007) Enhancing the quality of nursing care in methadone substitute clients using action research: a process evaluation. *Journal of Advanced Nursing* 422–431.

McLellan AT (2006) What we need is a system: Creating a responsive and effective substance abuse treatment system. In: W Miller & K Carroll (Eds) *Rethinking Substance Abuse.* Guildford Press: New York.

Mintzer M, Copersino M & Stitzer M (2005) Opioid abuse and cognitive performance, *Drug and Alcohol Dependence* **78** (5) 225–230.

National Institute for Health and Clinical Excellence (2007) *Drug Misuse: Psychosocial interventions.* London: NICE.

Newman R (1976) Methadone maintenance: It ain't what it used to be. *British Journal of Addiction* **71** 183–186.

Preble E & Casey J (1969) Taking care of business: The heroin user's life on the streets. *International Journal of the Addictions* **4** 1–24.

Prendergast M, Podus D, Chang E & Urada D (2002) The effectiveness of drug abuse treatment: a meta-analysis of comparison group studies. *Drug and Alcohol Dependence* **67** 53–72.

Robertson R, Bird S, Bruce M, Budd J, Carrieri M, Christie T, Cockayne L, Kastelic A, Fischer G, Gourlay D, Griffin S, Reisinger M, Kamarulzuman A, Lee S, McGoven G, MacLeod J, Kerr T, Nelles B, Newman R, Drucker E, Hickman M, Jay J, Joseph H, Malinowska-Sempruch K, Parnino M, Strang J, Ford C, Hall W, Roberts K, Shinderman M, Stolerman I, Uchtenhagen A, Ulmer A, Watson R, Van den Brink W, Wodak A, Wolf K, Wood E & Walcher S (2010) Methadone is key to effective drug treatment. *Scotsman* 5th April 2010.

Simpson DD (2004) A conceptual framework for drug treatment processes and outcomes. *Journal of Substance Abuse Treatment* **27** (2) 99–121.

Simpson D, Rowan-Szal G, Joe G, Best D, Day E & Campbell A (2009) Relating counsellor attributes to client engagement in England. *Journal of Substance Abuse Treatment* **36** 313–320.

Skipper G & Dupont R (2011) The physician health program: a replicable model of sustained recovery management. In: J Kelly & W White (Eds) *Addiction Recovery Management: Theory, research and practice*. Humana Press: Springer, New York.

White W (1990) *Pathways from the Culture of Addiction to the Culture of Recovery: A travel guide for addiction professionals*. Center City, Minnesota: Hazelden.

Wisely C (2010) Salford: towards a recovery-oriented city. *Safer Communities* **9** (4) 40–50.

Chapter 6

Recovery, social networks and contagion

The model presented in this book emphasises the central role of social networks in the stable recovery from addiction. This chapter explores this facet of recovery more thoroughly, starting with an overview of recent evidence about the core role of particular relationships before moving onto discuss the impact of social aspects of recovery, in particular the importance of recovery group membership and participation. However, the central focus of the chapter will be around an idea that has received considerable attention in the UK recently – that recovery is 'contagious' – drawing heavily on the work done on the Framingham Heart Study assessing the social spread of behaviours over time. Finally, it will explore the implications of enabling and supporting contagion spread in addiction recovery.

The evidence base supporting social components of addiction recovery

Integration with other people and the resulting social capital makes a difference to a person's recovery journey. Putnam (2000) concluded that *'the more integrated that we are with our community, the less likely we are to experience colds, heart attacks, strokes, cancer, depression and premature deaths of all sorts. Such protective effects have been confirmed for close family ties, for friendship networks, for participation in social events, and even for simple affiliation with religious and other civic associations'* (Putnam, 2000, p326). Putnam cites Berkman and Syme (1979) who reported that people with the fewest social ties have the highest risk of dying from heart disease, circulatory problems and cancer, even after controlling for social inequalities. This led Putnam to conclude that *'if you belong to no groups but decide to join one, you cut your risk of dying over the next year in half. If you smoke and belong to no groups, it's a toss-up statistically whether you should stop smoking or start joining'* (Putnam, 2000, p331).

The manifestation of this effect in addiction research is clear. Bond *et al* (2003) reported that individuals who had fewer drinkers in their social networks and more AA-based support for reducing drinking were more likely to initiate and maintain abstinence over a three-year interval. Similarly, Humphreys and Noke (1997) reported that there was something different about social networks that consisted primarily of AA members – they were typically better integrated and more supportive than networks consisting mainly of non-AA networks. Why should this be? Mohr *et al* (2001) found that friends and peers who have abstinence-focused behaviour help with the recovery process – alcohol treatment clients with more non-drinking friends at baseline were those who had more non-drinking friends at follow-up, which was associated with less drinking at the follow-up research interview.

In another study assessing recovery in drinkers, Beattie and Longabaugh (1999) found that short-term success in stopping drinking was associated with both higher levels of general support and, more specifically, friends' support for abstinence. They argued that the emotional and practical support offered by friends helps individuals who are trying to stop drinking to build up their self-confidence and to provide the practical assistance and companionship that people may need at such a difficult time.

This is even more true for intimate relationships. Moos (2011) claimed that individuals whose partners and close family members do not have substance-related problems are much more likely to remain abstinent and cites a study where patients whose partners did not use were twice as likely to be abstinent at one-year follow-up than those whose partners were drinking or using drugs (Tracy *et al*, 2005). Gogineni *et al* (2001) found that 83% of individuals whose partners and friends did not use substances were abstinent as opposed to only 34% of people whose partners and friends used. Thus, there is a clear relationship between intimate social networks – partners, family and friends – and the ability to stop using substances. The next section will extend this review to the benefits of being a member of a recovery group or community. Moos (2011) concludes that *'strong bonds with family members, especially a spouse or partner, who provide general support, goal direction, and supervision are associated with less substance use and a higher likelihood of abstinence'* (Moos, 2011, pp48–49).

The benefits of group membership

White (1990) argues that there are core benefits to being a member of a recovery group:

- emotional support – involving empathy, care, consideration, concern and encouragement

- informational support – providing knowledge about recovery and the recovery support services and groups available

- instrumental support – support in linking into supportive housing and childcare services, development of leisure and sporting activities and to recovery groups

- companionship

- validation – sharing and supporting recovery experiences.

In other words, belonging to a recovery group can be practical as well as emotionally supportive. This is entirely consistent with the notion of social capital advanced by Putnam (2000), among others, according to whom social networks constitute access to cherished resources, but in the case of recovery groups also provide the belief that recovery is possible and that it can be supported from within that forum. White (1990) goes further to suggest that recovery groups, in particular, can offer some key additional benefits:

- experience of acceptance and belonging

- build esteem through identification with a large organisation

- provide a belief system through which shame and defeat can be transformed into victory

- provide a vehicle for the safe discharge of powerful emotions

- provide a consistent set of rituals that facilitate emotional release and value-focusing

- provide a forum for consultation on daily problem-solving

- provide rituals that allow the group to celebrate success.

The recovery group is seen, therefore, to offer both belief systems and values that are shared and supportive but also that constitute a safe haven in which the individual can explore and grow. The idea that the social support system is the vehicle in which key aspects of personal recovery capital are developed (self-esteem, a sense of purpose, identity and belonging) is consistent with this model.

What are the mechanisms for social influence?

We will temporarily move away from research that focuses specifically on addiction to consider a research programme that has a profound influence on the understanding of social networks and their ability to mould and shape behaviour. The Framingham Heart Study is a cohort study that has followed a generation of adults from one American city every two to four years over a number of years using three primary sources – medical examinations, blood tests and a comprehensive questionnaire that focuses on social networks. Individuals are asked to list their friends by name so authors can match 'principals' with 'alters' and find out whether relationships are 'mutual' (with two individuals naming each other) or skewed (with only one individual naming the other as a friend).

The influence of social networks is illustrated in two key papers that focus on the spread of obesity and the widespread desistance from smoking in Framington (Christakis & Fowler, 2006; Christakis & Fowler, 2008). A person's odds of becoming obese increased by 57% if they had a friend who became obese, with a lower risk rate for friends of friends, lower again at three degrees of separation, and with no discernible effect at further levels of remove. In other words, there was not only a strong affect of friends' behaviour, but also of friends of friends and even friends of friends of friends. The same effect is shown with smoking. Smoking cessation by a spouse decreased a person's chances of smoking by 67%, while smoking cessation by a friend decreased the chances by 36%. The average risk of smoking at one degree of separation (ie. having a friend who smokes) was 61% higher, 29% higher at two degrees of separation and 11% higher at three degrees of separation.

In a follow-up study on binge drinking behaviour, Rosenquist *et al* (2010) reported that principals were 50% more likely to drink heavily if a person they are directly connected to drinks heavily; 36% more likely at two degrees of separation; and 15% at three degrees of separation. Conversely, people were 29% more likely to abstain if someone they are directly connected to abstained. This effect is 21% at two degrees of separation and five per cent at three degrees of separation. In other words, both the active engagement in the behaviour and its avoidance are linked to social activity.

In some ways, this is counter-intuitive – surely eating too much is a matter of personal behaviour, and obesity is fundamentally shaped by biology? A clue comes from *Connected: The amazing power of social networks and how they shape our lives*, a summary of findings from the Framingham Heart Study, in which Christakis and Fowler (2010) demonstrate the spread of divorce in Framingham. One of the core concepts in the model of contagion advanced by Christakis and Fowler is 'homophily' – the idea that we seek out people who are similar to us – and they suggest a clear 'peer selection' effect – that our social networks will reflect the values and beliefs we have. However, we are also shaped by our peer networks. For example, when friends stop smoking, the appeal of being the only smoker standing outside in the cold, missing out on conversation and returning to a group that complains about the effects of residual smoke on their clothes and hair, is a disincentive to smoke. By the same token, when work colleagues buy cakes on a Friday, go for takeaways at lunchtime and go to the pub regularly, we may well notice our weight going up.

The common pattern is that the behaviours of our peers, siblings and friends not only shapes our behaviour, but it also shapes how we see the world and the 'parameters' of possible behaviour. It is no coincidence that one of the key findings in the Framingham Heart Study is that the key predictor of contagion is social distance and not geographical distance. In other words, if you do not know your next door neighbours you will not be subject to contagion of their behaviours, but if you know them well, you will be. The implication of the Framingham Heart Study is that a huge diversity of behaviours are influenced by social networks, with stronger degrees of association predictive of greater likelihood of behaviour change. The advantage of multiple phases of data collection is that the studies have been able to show the direction of influence and to map changes in the behaviour of 'principals' against what happens to their social networks. This has shown that if you are increasingly exposed to smoking cessation, divorce or obesity among family, friends and colleagues, your own likelihood of these behaviours is considerably enhanced at the next assessment point, with the likelihood shaped by the number of links and their strength.

The other key issue that Christakis and Fowler demonstrated is that not all networks are equivalent and that people vary both in their network structure and in their place within social networks. Individuals vary in the extent to which they are parts of one or more networks. Some people will be members of several networks and others will have minimal social networks; people's roles within these networks will vary – they will either be central or peripheral to them. This will also apply to networks – if network members all know each other but do not know anyone else, the implications for contagion is much more limited than if there are networks of overlapping groups and social networks that are linked (see Figure 6.1).

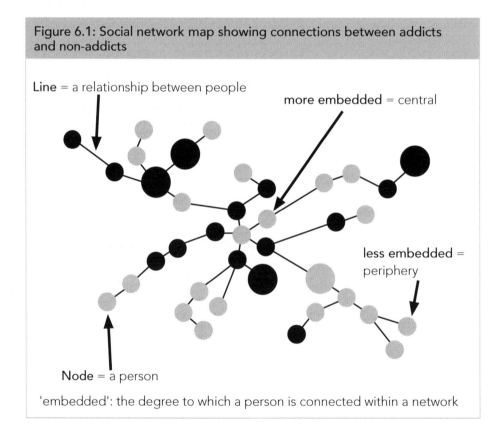

Figure 6.1: Social network map showing connections between addicts and non-addicts

Line = a relationship between people

more embedded = central

less embedded = periphery

Node = a person

'embedded': the degree to which a person is connected within a network

In Figure 6.1, the black dots represent addicts and the grey dots represent non-addicts. The cluster of black dots at the centre of the map are the individuals who are central to the overall network and so central to the notion of contagion and change in social patterns. It is important to

Addiction Recovery: A movement for social change and personal growth in the UK ©
Pavilion Publishing (Brighton) Ltd 2012

remember that behaviour change can happen in both directions – there are both epidemics of addictive behaviour as well as periods and places where recovery is contagious. The factors that determine this are not entirely understood but there are important lessons to be learnt from social network maps.

The first is about specialist treatments including, but not restricted to, inpatient and residential rehabilitation. No matter how good the treatment and how strong the person's intentions, if a person in the early stages of recovery (a newly converted grey dot in Figure 6.1) is returned to a community and a social network consisting only of black dots (representing active addicts), then this person will be at high risk of relapse, particularly if the specialist intervention does not actively and assertively link the person into groups of supportive white dots. The reason this is not a simple question of numbers is about the size and nature of the dot – we are not all equal. The attractiveness of returning to the social network of addicts is in competition with the recovery capital resources the person returning from treatment has at their disposal, but the probability of maintaining recovery will reflect both the person's ability to avoid social engagement with the black nodes and networks and their ability to seek out the support and membership of non-addict networks.

The implication of this is clear – to use White's (1990) language, the transition from the culture of addiction to the culture of recovery is crucial as it changes not only who people spend their time with, but also what they do with their time, what options are available for things to do and how they see the world. Changing the social groups a person engages in changes what they do with their time, what they consider to be 'normal' and acceptable behaviour, the language they use and as a result, what their world looks and feels like. The social world defines identity and meaning, self-perception and the repertoire of words and actions that are available to people. As most people will have the option to move from group to group, and from networks of addiction to networks of recovery, the crucial predictor of a social safety net is its capacity to offer more attractive role models, activities and belief systems than those that characterised addiction careers. This is a tall order, and one that will be returned to in discussing the idea of champions of recovery. However, the same principles apply to recovery groups and communities – they are up against a powerful and entrenched magnet, and they must offer enough that is meaningful and attractive so that individuals will not only be drawn, but will not want to leave once they are involved.

Can we influence social networks to change addictive behaviour?

There is a danger that this results in a fatalism on the part of recovery groups and services based on the belief that people will only engage in such activities and groups when they are 'ready', and that this readiness is a maturational process that each person will come to in their own time. The following evidence from research trials and 'assertive linkage' studies suggests that this is open to intervention, if the appropriate agents of change and supports are involved. Litt *et al* (2007) assessed the benefits of randomising people to 'network support'. They found that, of 186 participants randomised to network support (NS), case management (CM) or network support plus contingency management (NS+CM), participants in both network support conditions had better outcomes than case management alone. Litt *et al* (2007) found that *'the addition of just one abstinent person to a social network increased the probability of abstinence for the next year by 27%'.*

In a follow-up to this study in 2009, Litt *et al* (2009) reported two-year post-treatment outcomes in 210 alcohol-dependent men and women randomised as above to network support (with or without contingency management) or case management. The network support-only condition yielded up to 20% more days abstinent at two years than either of the other conditions. Litt *et al* (2009) also found that changes in social networks to include others in recovery were associated with increases in self-efficacy and coping that were strongly linked to better drinking outcomes. Most of the positive network changes were linked to 12-step attendance, leading the authors to conclude that *'AA attendance and increasing the number of non-drinking friends in the social network were strong (direct and indirect) predictors of outcome, appearing to result in increased abstinence in part due to the effects on self-efficacy'* (Litt *et al*, 2009, p241).

A key finding from this study is the idea that we do not need to be passive in waiting for individuals to migrate from addiction-focused to recovery-focused social networks. Active engagement and encouragement of engaging with individuals in recovery (primarily through mutual aid groups in Litt's studies) had a profound effect on their social networks and on their likelihood of abstinence. Another key finding is that social change provides the space and the support that allows individuals to develop the personal recovery capital (in this case, self-efficacy) that is critical to the recovery process.

Timko *et al* (2005) found that this effect is also seen in terms of linkage to mutual aid groups while in treatment. In the study, participants were encouraged to attend mutual aid groups in one of three ways – 1) by providing them with leaflets promoting 12-step groups, 2) by a doctor discussing it with them and encouraging them to attend and 3) by peers meeting them and taking them to their first meetings. While there were some enhanced levels of attendance in both doctor and peer conditions – and both were associated not only with better meeting attendance, but better drinking outcomes – it was peer support that had the greatest effect on attendance. Thus, not only is it possible for the likelihood of engagement to be influenced by interventions, this has been shown to lead to better engagement post-discharge and better abstinence outcomes.

Social networks – conclusions

The evidence outlined in this chapter has profound implications both for understanding addiction and what can be done to intervene in this process. As Orford (2008) argues, addiction science has focused disproportionately on the technical aspects of treatment – medication one compared to medication two, psychological intervention A versus psychological intervention B – leading to a very narrow and professionalised model of 'what works' in addiction, with far too little attention paid to what goes on outside the clinic in the daily routines and social practices of those seeking help.

Recovery is embedded in social networks. The author has now collected over 1,000 recovery stories in the UK and in none of these has recovery occurred in isolation. Recovery is first social, and then contagious. Other people demonstrate that recovery is possible and will provide the techniques and supports that provide the protection and the sense of identity and belonging that allow individuals the opportunity to develop the esteem, confidence, coping skills, sense of identity and sense of purpose that make sustained recovery a possibility. They also provide the sense of direction and belonging that individuals can either embed themselves in or grow out of. And, as we will explore in subsequent chapters, it is that sub-group who are both able to be visible as being in recovery and who give back as part of their recovery journey who create the possibility of contagion and who can challenge stereotypes and stigma.

Key learning points

■ Family members and friends have a profound effect on treatment and recovery success. If partners and friends are ongoing users, risk is increased, if they are also in recovery or non-users, the chance of relapse is reduced.

■ People acquire many behaviours through social learning (by watching others) and what they do is profoundly shaped by the activities of their friends and acquaintances.

■ This is made clear in the Framingham Heart Study, which has shown how all kinds of behaviour – including binge drinking and smoking cessation – but also obesity and divorce – are shaped by social networks.

■ The key implication is that by enabling changes in social networks, we can change the likelihood that people will sustain sobriety.

■ 'Assertive linkage' to groups in active recovery has a strong and positive effect on recovery likelihood.

References

Beattie M & Longabaugh R (1999) General and alcohol-specific social support following treatment. *Addictive Behaviours* **24** 593–606.

Berkman L & Syme S (1979) Social networks, host resistance and mortality: a nine-year follow-up of Alameda County residents. *The American Journal of Epidemiology* **109** 186–204.

Bond J, Kaskutas L & Weisner C (2003) The persistent influence of social networks and Alcoholics Anonymous on abstinence. *Journal of Studies on Alcohol* **64** 579–588.

Christakis NA & Fowler JH (2006) The spread of obesity in a large social network over 32 years. *New England Journal of Medicine* **357** (4) 370–379.

Christakis NA & Fowler JH (2008) The collective dynamics of smoking in a large social network. *New England Journal of Medicine* **358** (21) 2249–2258.

Christakis N & Fowler J (2010) *Connected: The amazing power of social networks and how they shape our lives.* London: Harper Press.

Gogineni A, Stein M & Friedmann P (2001) Social relationships and intravenous drug use among methadone maintenance patients. *Drug and Alcohol Dependence* **64** 47–53.

Humphreys K & Noke J (1997) Individual and social benefits of mutual aid self-help groups. *Social Policy* **27** 12–19.

Litt M, Kadden R, Kabela-Cormier E & Petry N (2007) Changing network support for drinking: Initial findings from the network support project. *Journal of Consulting and Clinical Psychology* **75** 542–555.

Litt M, Kadden R, Kabela-Cormier E & Petry N (2009) Changing network support for drinking: Network support projects 2-year follow-ups. *Journal of Consulting and Clinical Psychology* **77** (2) 229–242.

Mohr C, Averne S, Kenny D & Del Boca F (2001) Getting by (or getting high) with a little help from my friends: An examination of adults' alcohol friendships. *Journal of Studies on Alcohol* **62** 637–645.

Moos R (2011) Processes that promote recovery from addictive disorders. In: J Kelly & W White (Eds) *Addiction Recovery Management: Theory, Research and Practice.* New York: Humana Press Springer.

Orford J (2008) Asking the right questions the right way: the need for a shift in research on psychological treatments for addiction. *Addiction* **103** 875–887.

Putnam R (2000) *Bowling Alone: The collapse and revival of the American community.* New York: Simon and Schuster.

Rosenquist J, Murabito J, Fowler J & Christakis N (2010) The spread of alcohol consumption behaviour in a large social network. *Annals of Internal Medicine* **152** (7) 426–433.

Timko C, Dixon, K & Moos RH (2005) Treatment for Dual Diagnosis Patients in the Psychiatric and Substance Abuse Systems. *Mental Health Services Research* **7** (4) 229–242.

Tracy S, Kelly J & Moos R (2005) The influence of partner status, relationship quality and relationship stability on outcomes following intensive substance use disorder treatment. *Journal of Studies on Alcohol* **66** 497–505.

White W (1990) *Pathways from the Culture of Addiction to the Culture of Recovery: A travel guide for addiction professionals.* Center City, MN: Hazelden.

Chapter 7

Recovery and public policy

Public policy matters, as Babor *et al* (2010) argue, although they point out that the evidence base for drug policy at a national and international level is limited. In both Scotland and England, national strategies and local implementation plans have had a profound influence on the configuration of services, the dominant philosophies of treatment and the relative impact and input of a range of professional groups. Although there is often consensus that what is offered is a bio-psycho-social model of intervention, with significant user involvement and personalised choice, there has been a dominance of medical and psychiatric hegemony that has rarely been challenged. There is some growing recognition that tokenistic attempts at user involvement are not sufficient and that active ownership of the agenda and its resulting knowledge base are fundamental to the success of a recovery approach. The current strategies in England and Scotland offer a challenge to that model – and the resulting hierarchy of knowledge and decision making – but one that will be time-limited and that is not guaranteed to succeed. This chapter provides an overview of the current policies in Scotland and England. It places the policies in a historical context before critically reviewing where that leaves us and what this means for the implementation of recovery models and systems.

Scotland: The Road to Recovery

In Scotland, the focus of drug strategy is explicitly on recovery since the publication of *The Road to Recovery: A new approach to tackling Scotland's drug problem* (Scottish Government, 2008), which produced a number of definitions for recovery, including *'a process through which an individual is enabled to move from their problem drug use, towards a drug-free lifestyle as an active and contributing member of society'* (Scottish Government, 2008, pvi). Inspired by the perceived success of the Scottish Recovery Network for mental health, the executive summary of the document goes on to assert that *'Moving to an approach that is based on recovery will mean a significant change in both the pattern of services that are commissioned and in the way that practitioners engage with individuals'* (Scottish Government, 2008, pvi). There is also a recognition that this is an individualised process: *'Recovery is about helping an individual to achieve their full potential – with the ultimate goal being what is important to the individual, rather than the means by which it is achieved'* (Scottish Government, 2008, p23). However, in the strategy there was no action plan or operationalisation of any of the recovery objectives. Although it established a national support function, and required a stock-take of local partnerships for delivery, there were no targets set for recovery or for any of the other areas highlighted in the strategy.

As with mental health, much of the responsibility for implementation was devolved to a new organisation – the Scottish Drugs Recovery Consortium (SDRC) – set up under the strategy with the aim of working with the local commissioning systems (Alcohol and Drug Partnerships) to implement recovery approaches and models. In the strategy it is initially termed a 'drugs recovery network'. The SDRC was provided with £300,000 to establish itself as an independent charity that would work with the Scottish Government in implementing recovery processes and practices. Following the launch of the strategy, the Scottish Government also commissioned a review of the evidence base around recovery (Best *et al*, 2010), which included a research framework to specify key areas for development and supported the contention that recovery is an evidence-based approach, although the overall amount of both recovery research and clinical research in Scotland was extremely limited. The aim of the review was to identify the key gaps in knowledge that could potentially be addressed locally. One conclusion was that there was insufficient infrastructure or human resources in Scotland to provide the evidence base for such an ambitious agenda.

At the time of writing, the Scottish strategy is now three years old and there is little evidence of coherent or consistent implementation across the 30 Alcohol and Drug Partnership (ADP) areas in Scotland. While there has been a shift in language, and a general increase in awareness around the concept of recovery, its impact is hard to assess. This is partly because the strategy set no clear targets – how many people should move from treatment to recovery, or indeed what impact should there be on the number of people in treatment? The definitions provided in the Scottish strategy are not sufficiently exact that they lend themselves to simple enumeration and there remains the problem of 'medicated recovery' and what proportion of the estimated 20,000 individuals receiving opiate substitute prescriptions in Scotland should be classed as 'in recovery' or indeed as 'recovered' (McKeganey, 2011).

At around the same time that the recovery strategy was launched, HEAT targets were established in health services in Scotland and were essentially around waiting times for drug treatment. HEAT is an acronym for: Health improvement for the people of Scotland; Efficiency and governance improvements; Access to services; Treatment appropriate to individuals. The specific aims were *'to agree a target to offer individuals with problem drug use faster access to appropriate treatment to support their recovery'* and that *'by March 2013, 90% of clients will wait no longer than three weeks from referral received to appropriate drug treatment that supports their recovery'*. While this has focused much of the attention of service providers on a tangible set of performance indicators that are absent around the measurement of recovery, it also further establishes the centrality of specialist treatment services as the mechanism for delivering recovery.

One of the major concerns with implementing a recovery agenda in Scotland, in contrast to England, is around the commissioning processes and the central role of the NHS. In England there is a much clearer separation of the commissioning and the provision of drug services, with drug action teams (DATs) acting as oversight partnerships who commission and review packages of services, and where there is no preferred provider. As a consequence, a number of areas no longer have a mental health trust or NHS services at the heart of the system. In contrast, in Scotland the funding structures for drug services are through NHS providers and so there is no possibility of de-commissioning of the NHS part of the treatment systems in the Alcohol and Drug Partnerships that are the Scottish equivalents of the English DATs. Thus, the leverage towards changes in systems have not been driven in the same way by commissioning as discussed below, after the overview of the English system.

Another important contrast that is apparent in Scotland with the HEAT targets is around the issue of measurement. While waiting times can be measured relatively easily, meaning that performance can be managed by services and commissioners, the idea of measuring recovery and recovery-oriented systems is much more complex. Underlying this problem is a lack of clarity of what recovery looks like or even where or how it should be measured. There are some core concerns about what should be measured.

1. People in recovery may not be accessible or available for assessing their functioning either because they never accessed treatment services or, having done so, are moving on with their lives. So counting people in recovery is difficult.

2. If people are accessible, what is measured? The definitional issues in Chapter 1 suggest that recovery is a long-term process, is personal and will change over time. It is also complicated by the difficulty of reconciling potentially 'objective' indicators – abstinence, employment status, and so on – with 'subjective' measures of well-being, quality of life and a sense of belonging.

3. There is a second level of assessment that is about service delivery of recovery approaches and models. It is not clear whether increasing or decreasing numbers in treatment would be a sign of recovery success, or whether measures such as successful treatment exits or lower rates of treatment re-admission would be indicative of recovery success.

One of the major challenges for the recovery movement is to work out its 'metrics' – what should be expected of recovery-oriented services or systems, and how to know if these aims are being delivered. It is easy to criticise the Scottish Government for failing to measure or performance-manage the recovery activities of each of the 30 alcohol and drug partnerships while doing so for treatment waiting times, but the field has to achieve a consensus on what would be measured and what benefits this would confer. This question will be returned to after reviewing the situation and process in England.

England: Drug Strategy 2010 – Reducing demand, restricting supply, building recovery: Supporting people to live a drug free life

In 2008, the Home Office in England published the UK drug strategy *Drugs: Protecting families and communities – 2008–2018* (Home Office, 2008), which set out four primary areas: protecting communities through tackling supply; crime and anti-social behaviour; preventing harm to children and young people; delivering new approaches to drug treatment and social re-integration and public information campaigns, communications and community engagement. Yet only two years later the above strategy was launched with a foreword from the Home

Secretary Teresa May asserting its differentiation from its predecessors: *'A fundamental difference between this strategy and those that have gone before is that instead of focusing primarily on reducing the harms caused by drug misuse, our approach will be to go much further and offer every support for people to choose recovery as an achievable way out of dependency'* (HM Government, 2010, p2).

The body of the document also focuses on change, talking of a *'fundamentally different approach to tackling drugs and an entirely new ambition to reduce drug use and dependence'* (HM Government, 2010, p3). The role of recovery has thus gained momentum and is considerably more overt. The document calls for the generation of recovery champions at a community, therapeutic and strategic level within a 'whole systems approach'. There is an increasing recognition of the community as the key locale for recovery activity and the explicit recognition that *'recovery can be contagious'* (HM Government, 2010, p21).

Not only is there a section on recovery (and not a section of the strategy specifically focused on treatment), there is a recognition of a much wider definition of inclusion – the strategy explicitly endorses *'active promotion and support of local mutual aid networks such as Alcoholics and Narcotics Anonymous'* (HM Government, 2010, p21). The strategy is suffused with recovery language and discusses the role of community, the role of 'recovery champions' and the need for ongoing supports to enable employment and sober living housing.

Yet the problems that exist in Scotland also arise in England – the responsibility for implementation is devolved to a local level and with nothing in the document that provides methods of measuring whether the recovery approach has been successfully implemented. The difference in commissioning approaches and systems does mean there is one fundamental difference – there is more power devolved to local commissioners to de-commission providers, including NHS providers who do not show sufficient transition from an acute care to a recovery-oriented approach.

There is also a shift in 'ownership' of the English drug strategy with the closure of the National Treatment Agency for Substance Use (NTA, see below) and its functions passing over to Public Health England (PHE). In this new system, directors of public health will have commissioning and oversight of drug (and alcohol) treatment and recovery as a core part of their work, and this is to be aligned and managed locally. The strategy emphasises an 'outcome focused' approach:

- *'freedom from dependence on drugs or alcohol*

- *prevention of drug related deaths and bloodborne viruses*

- *a reduction in crime and re-offending*

- *sustained employment*

- *the ability to access and sustain suitable accommodation*

- *improvement in mental and physical health and well-being*

- *improved relationships with family members, partners and friends*

- *the capacity to be an effective and caring parent'.*

(HM Government, 2010, p21).

One of the core mechanisms for delivery is based on the idea that 'money will follow success' with the system reconfigured so that there are incentives for delivering recovery outcomes. Part of this work will see six Payment by Results pilot projects and it will be crucial that these projects develop a consensus about what is to be delivered and how success will be measured.

Why are the recovery strategies different, and why are they needed? A brief historical overview

The following is not meant to be a comprehensive history as it has been reported in a number of other works on drug treatment. The detail is summarised in *Heroin Addiction and The British System* – a key text edited by Strang and Gossop (2005). A brief review of the author's own experiences as head of research for the National Treatment Agency, work on developing the 2008 drug strategy, work on a priority review of drug treatment for the Prime Minister's Delivery Unit and ongoing involvement in policy and research with both Scottish and English governments follows.

Prior to the starting point for this discussion, with the advent of early HIV cases in the mid-1980s, there are generally considered to be two primary phases in UK drug treatment. The first of these, the 'British system', largely ended by the advent of a more regulatory framework, heralded by the advent of drug-related HIV and reinforced by the drugs and crime agenda. The 'British system' dominated up until the early 1970s with a primarily health-driven focus and a central role for general practitioners. Indeed, Strang and Gossop (2005) speak of a new type of heroin user that emerged in the 1980s, related to social disadvantage, lack of opportunity and where heroin use was a standard part of daily activity. Berridge (2005) argues, in her contribution to the book, that there really was no such thing as a British system, rather a liberal model of inactivity, justified on the basis that there was no real problem for policymakers to deal with. That changed with the advent of primarily white, male, working class heroin use in the 1980s with the resultant concerns about the spread of HIV, dependence-fuelled criminality and the impact on urban communities.

The model that dominated was a personal health model and did not reflect the dominance of the criminal justice approach that had dominated in the US in the equivalent period with the Harrison Act and its ramifications. This changed only slightly in the 1970s with a growing addiction specialism, made manifest in the form of the 'drug dependency units' (DDUs) that emerged in this period in the large urban centres in response, primarily, to a growth in amphetamine and hallucinogenic drug use and problems. Although more specialised, the model was still mainly a health one and the aim was around addressing issues of personal well-being, but this was still prior to the growth of heroin use among the urban, working class communities described above.

The advent of the initial cases of drug-related HIV were a dramatic culmination of a growing concern about the emergence of heroin use in urban centres in the UK. The discovery by Dr Roy Robertson, a GP from Muirhouse in Edinburgh, that around half of his known injecting drug users were HIV positive led to a dramatic shift in response and policy (see Table 7.1) (Robertson & Richardson, 2007).

Table 7.1: What do we want from treatment – recovery as a new form of outcome

Dates and models	Locus of control
Up to 1985: 'The British system'	Autonomous power of the general practitioner
1985 – 1998: The public health system	Public health measured by dissemination of disease
2001 – 2007: The managerialist model	Bureaucratisation and the dominance of front-end targets
2007 – now: The renaissance of the recovery movement	Shift in locus to the individual and in targets to families, communities and quality of life

In the period after the advent of the initial cases of HIV, there was a substantial increase in funding for early interventions and the advent of a harm reduction movement, which was much less concerned with stopping individuals from using, but focused more on reducing the harms accrued by the user and by wider society. From our perspective, what is crucial about the harm reduction model and the advent of HIV is the change it brought about in the measurement of 'success' in drug treatment. At the most basic level the aim of interventions switched from personal health to public health, and the success of the new harm reduction models was judged on its impact on the spread of AIDS and subsequently, other blood-borne viruses. Stimson and Lart (2005) describe three principal changes in drug policy in the UK in the 1980s. First, the purely medical perspective on drug use and drug users was challenged; second, there was considerable fragmentation in the delivery of treatment services at a local level; and, third, there was an increased centralism as the 'liberal inactivity' of previous generations was replaced with increased central government control and funding of interventions.

In the second volume of *Heroin Addiction and the British System* (Strang & Gossop, 2005), Gruer (2005) describes the public health response in Glasgow. Following a Scottish Office report in 1994, the first Glasgow Drug Action Team strategy appeared in 1995 and focused on reducing the sharing of injecting equipment, reducing the prevalence and frequency of injecting, and reducing the extent of drug misuse. The central plank for delivering this was the establishment of a methadone prescribing scheme overseen by the Glasgow Drug Problem Service (GDPS) but delivered in large part through GP practices (by 1999 more than 130 had signed up across the city). Although Gruer concludes that the initiative had succeeded in preventing an epidemic, he argues that *'it is unlikely that much overall improvement will be possible without substantial regeneration of deprived areas and the creation of worthwhile employment opportunities for the young people who live there'* (Gruer, 2005, p165).

The next major transition came about as a result of the successes of the newly expanding drug treatment services emerging in the UK. The then Conservative Government commissioned the National Treatment Outcome Research Study to assess what worked in drug treatment (Gossop *et al*, 1998). The unequivocal support for treatment (as reviewed in Chapter 4) also led to a major finding that was of particular importance to policy-makers – the impact of drug treatment on crime, particularly acquisitive crime in the form of shoplifting, car crime, burglaries and fraud (Gossop *et al,* 1998). As with the link between HIV and drug use, so the link between crime and drug use prompted another huge injection of cash into drug treatment with the promise of marked reductions in offending behaviour. In England, this led to nationwide attempts to divert drug users into treatment at the point of arrest (via schemes known as Testing on Arrest and the Drug Intervention Programme), at the point of sentencing (via Drug Treatment and Testing Orders, subsequently renamed Drug Rehabilitation Requirements) and during time spent in prison (in the form of the counselling, assessment, referral, advice and through care teams). This huge investment of new structures and resources also led to a shift in departmental ownership of drug treatment with the Home Office playing an increasing role and a further and extremely significant shift in target setting. By this time, the newly ramped up drug services across the country had targets that related to reducing the spread of disease and to the reduction in the levels of acquisitive crime.

This newly industrialised approach was overseen by the creation of a new body – the National Treatment Agency for Substance Misuse (NTA). The NTA was established in London and had nine regional offices. This structure was further bureaucratised by the division of the nine regions into 149 Drug Action Teams (subsequently many of these would merge into Crime and Disorder Reduction Partnerships and Drug and Alcohol Action Teams), with the goal of the new system summed up in the strapline 'More treatment. Better treatment. Fairer treatment' (National Treatment Agency, 2001). The job of this new hierarchy was to oversee the treatment systems and the linked specialist budgets – known in England as the pooled treatment budget (PTB). The new agency not only issues guidance on how treatment systems should work (a national service framework was first published in 2002 and then updated in 2006 [National Treatment Agency, 2002; National Treatment Agency, 2006]), but also provided a forum for the targets set.

The primary focus of the new treatment system was around access, with three broad areas of targeting – one of the targets for the new treatment system was to double the numbers accessing specialist treatment between 1998 and 2008; to reduce waiting times to a maximum of three weeks across all the service modalities; and finally, to ensure that clients accessing specialist community treatments would be retained for at least 12 weeks. Each Drug Action Team area was set a target percentage for each of these measures and this was duly passed down to the commissioned providers of services.

One unanticipated consequence of this model was to create a 'house with a front door and no back door'. In other words, providers and commissioners were incentivised only to attract drug users into treatment and to keep them there, and were not encouraged to support them to come out the other end. This caused resources to become stretched and a reduction in the quality of provision as more and more clients were recruited into a limited set of treatment options, most typically based on maintenance substitution prescriptions with little adequate incentives or supports to allow service users to move on and through treatment (Best *et al,* 2009; Wisely, 2010).

However, this model has been superseded in England by two developments – the first is the shift in policy and philosophy from a 'treatment and harm reduction' model to a recovery model, and the second around the commissioning models used. The growth in numbers in treatment was not seen as either sufficient or sufficiently successful in reducing crime, mortality or disease. The shift in commissioning required all services to be open to competitive tendering by removing the exclusivity of the NHS and mental health trusts as the primary providers of drug treatment in England – a change that has not occurred in Scotland.

The gap between policy and practice: a hypothesis about national differences

This is the most contentious section of the chapter and one that the author has struggled to write. In spite of the Scottish strategy mentioned previously, and the establishment of the Scottish Drugs Recovery Consortium, it appears that there is considerably more recovery innovation in English treatment than in its Scottish equivalent. Why should this be the case? It is not the same as claiming that there is a shortage of community-level recovery initiatives or even an extremely strong mutual aid movement in Scotland, but in terms of embedding recovery within a treatment system, there is greater evidence that this is already happening in England than in Scotland, and the suggested reason for this is the relative position of commissioners and NHS service providers in the two countries.

In England, where the re-tendering of NHS services and the removal of their privileged position in the competitive marketplace has been established for a number of years now, local commissioners have had the scope and the authority to implement recovery models, and where providers have resisted this approach, both the threat of de-commissioning and its ultimate implementation have enabled change to be driven through local systems. There is also a more robust database (using the National Drug Treatment Monitoring System) to ensure that the desired outcome – 'treatment completed, drug-free' can be monitored at both a locality level and a service delivery level. Although problems of operationalisation are as problematic in England as in Scotland, the differences in commissioning arrangements have ensured that where there is a commitment (either at Drug Action Team or regional level) to recovery approaches, the commissioners have the tools to ensure that this is carried through. Chapters 9–11 will review what this has meant in practical terms and the resulting innovations.

By contrast, in Scotland there has been no change in the way that services are commissioned and so the locality drug and alcohol budgets are directly under the control of the mainstream health providers. In the Scottish strategy, the final section of the *Road to Recovery: A new approach to tackling Scotland's drug problem* (Scottish Government, 2008) is an action plan for delivering outcomes. For the outcome *'to facilitate people moving on and recovering from problem drug use'*, the action is for *'health boards to review local service arrangements in relation to local services, including pharmacies, to ensure that they offer flexible access to service provision allowing people with problem drug use to attend work, education and employment'* (Scottish Government, 2008, p72). It should be evident from previous chapters that conferring recovery is not the responsibility of health services or boards, and that the fundamental principles of empowerment, co-production and community and peer-based services and decision-making are fundamentally challenged by a model in which health providers are the primary 'facilitators' of community recovery. It remains to be seen if the Scottish Drugs Recovery Consortium will be able to address this problem, but it is a major concern that the recovery agenda is basically in the hands of health boards whose financial and vested interests may be challenged by fully embracing a recovery model.

Overview and conclusions

The evolution of drug policy in the UK has gathered momentum in recent years and, despite devolution, both Scotland and England have produced drug strategies that are radical and consistent in their commitment to a recovery model. This is a huge challenge to commissioners, service managers and workers who are faced with a new philosophy and paradigm, yet will also be faced with many of the same clients who have been attending during the last decade when a managerialist model of engagement and retention dominated. This creates a huge human resource and training conundrum for commissioners and services, particularly as the academic and policy field have not yet developed sufficiently robust measurement tools to assess effective recovery progress for individuals, services or localities.

As Babor *et al* (2010) argue, there are three broad categories of instrument available to policymakers to assess the quality of policy endeavours – systems for credentialing workers and services; process indicators of performance; and outcome monitoring systems. The authors cited work by Smith *et al* (1980) based on a meta-analysis of hundreds of studies that concluded that training has no impact on counselling outcomes. Babor *et al* (1980) concluded that process performance measures may be the most useful method available in the absence of adequate outcome indicators.

Yet this remains an incredible opportunity, based on the vision and foresight of politicians and policymakers to transform dated treatment processes with recovery models that can offer hope, choice and belief to individuals, families and communities. The next section of the book starts to examine how those local models have started to evolve and where the examples of hope and success are being modelled.

Key learning points

■ Policymakers in both England and Scotland have produced national drug policies that have paved the way for real change towards a recovery philosophy.

■ In both countries, the policies make explicit calls on specialist services to transform their ways of working to embrace recovery approaches and thinking.

■ However, both lack detail on how this will be achieved and in England the operationalisation of recovery models is decentralised to local areas and partnerships.

■ In Scotland, the implementation of recovery approaches has had major success but has been geographically patchy and is not underpinned by a clear and consistent evaluation framework.

■ The successful implementation of recovery models will require the development of clear metrics for assessing and evaluating how success is identified and quantified.

References

Babor T, Caulkins J, Edwards G, Fischer B, Foxcroft D, Humphreys K, Obot I, Rehm J, Reuter P, Room R, Rossow I & Strang J (2010) *Drug Policy and the Public Good*. Oxford: Oxford University Press.

Berridge V (2005) The British System and its history: myth and reality. In: J Strang & M Gossop (Eds) *Heroin Addiction and the British System: Volume 1: Origins and evolution*. Abingdon, Oxon: Routledge.

Best D, Day E, Morgan B, Oza T, Copello A & Gossop M (2009) What treatment means in practice: An analysis of the therapeutic activity provided in criminal justice drug treatment services in Birmingham, England. *Addiction Research and Theory* **17** (6) 678–687.

Best D, Rome A, Hanning K, White W, Gossop M, Taylor A & Perkins A (2010) *Research for Recovery: A review of the drugs evidence base. Crime and Justice Social Research, Scottish Government*. Edinburgh: Scottish Government.

Gossop M, Marsden J & Stewart D (1998) *NTORS at One Year: Changes in substance use, health and criminal behaviour one year after intake*. London: Department of Health.

Gruer L (2005) *The Emergence of City-wide Public Health Responses to the Drugs Problem. Heroin addiction and the British System: Volume 2: Treatment and policy responses*. Abingdon, Oxon: Routledge.

HM Government (2010) *Drug Strategy 2010 – Reducing demand, restricting supply, building recovery: Supporting people to live a drug free life*. London: HM Government.

Home Office (2008) *Drugs: Protecting families and communities*. London: Home Office.

McKeganey N (2011) *Controversies in Drug Policy and Race*. New York: Palgrave McMillan.

National Treatment Agency (2001) *Models of Care for Adult Substance Misusers*. London: NTA.

National Treatment Agency (2002) *Models of Care*. London: NTASM.

National Treatment Agency (2006) *Models of Care: Update*. London: NTASM.

Robertson R & Richardson A (2007) Heroin injecting and the introduction of HIV/AIDS into a Scottish city. *Journal of the Royal Society of Medicine* **100** 491–494.

Scottish Government (2008) *The Road to Recovery: A new approach to tackling Scotland's drug problem*. Edinburgh: Scottish Government.

Scottish Office (1994) *Drug Misuse in Scotland. Meeting the challenge: Report of a Ministerial Drugs Task Force*. Edinburgh: HMSO.

Smith M, Glass G & Miller T (1980) *The Benefits of Psychotherapy*. Baltimore, MD: John Hopkins University Press.

Stimson G & Lart R (2005) *The Relationship between the State and Local Practice in the Development of National Policy on Drugs between 1920 and 1990. Heroin addiction and the British System: Volume 1: Origins and evolution*. Abingdon, Oxon: Routledge.

Strang J & Gossop M (2005) *Heroin Addiction and the British System: Volume 1: Origins and evolution*. Abingdon, Oxon: Routledge.

Wisely C (2010) Salford: towards a recovery oriented city. *Safer Communities* **9** (4) 40–50.

Chapter 8

Recovery-oriented systems of care

This chapter examines the implementation of policy at a local level. While there is limited evidence about the effectiveness of policy at a national level (Babor *et al,* 2010), evidence presented in a review by Smart and Mann (2000) suggests that increases in both AA membership and professionally provided services are associated with decreased rates of alcohol problems. In some countries the impact of this is large enough to reduce hospital admissions and liver cirrhosis deaths. Klingemann *et al* (1992) defined 'systems' in this context as the interconnection of different agencies, programmes and referrals channels that provide supporting services. It is this model, at local area level, that the chapter focuses on.

It is necessary to begin with an overview of the principles of 'recovery-oriented systems of care' before examining the evidence base for implementation in a number of US cities and regions. Edinburgh is focused on as a city that has seen an explosion of recovery activity based around two key hubs. The final section of the chapter reviews the lessons from the Edinburgh experience, of developing and generating recovery communities and systems in Scotland.

Principles of a recovery-oriented system

The Centre for Substance Abuse Treatment (CSAT) identified 17 principles of recovery-orientated care systems in *Guiding Principles and Elements of Recovery-Oriented Systems of Care: What do we know from the research?* The principles are:

- there are many pathways to recovery
- person-centred
- inclusive of family and other ally involvement

- individualised and comprehensive services across the lifespan
- systems anchored in the community
- continuity of care
- partnership–consultant relationships
- strengths based
- responsive to personal belief systems
- commitment to peer recovery support services
- inclusion of the voices and experiences of recovering individuals and their families
- integrated services
- system-wide education and training
- ongoing monitoring and outreach
- outcomes driven
- research based
- adequately and flexibly financed.

The report attempts to evidence each of these points, for instance providing the evidence that recovery-oriented support may foster greater self-efficacy and longer abstinence (Finney *et al,* 1998). Similarly, the report cites evidence that *'employment and stable housing have been found to improve self-esteem and support reintegration into mainstream society and thereby to support recovery'* (CSAT, 2009, p24). Although focusing on peer and community-focused activities, the report is keen to emphasise the importance of the bridges to formal treatment interventions and the importance of therapeutic activities and relationships. It cites two studies which reported that a positive therapeutic relationship can counteract the adverse effects of low initial self-efficacy and motivation (Ilgen *et al,* 2006a; Ilgen *et al,* 2006b). The authors also cite White (2007) discussing a 'recovery revolution' in Philadelphia, where services made significant changes to clinical practices around engagement, retention, assessment, the role of the client, service relationships, clinical care, service intensity and duration, the sites for delivering services, post-treatment check-ups and supports and attitudes towards re-admission.

Overall, the model that emerges from the CSAT report is one of fundamentally shifting treatment services and processes by focusing on continuity of care; client empowerment and ownership of the treatment process; and clinical work that is based on strengths not deficits, and that this change in philosophy and practice applies across entire systems not merely in segments of them. For many services, this is not a gradual process of evolution but a radical change in both the philosophy and practice of drug treatment. And, crucially, it will rely much less on activities that take place within specialist centres of treatment and will involve more community-focused activities that are enabled by families and peers in community settings.

Examples of recovery success in North America

British Columbia

Drug Dependence Treatment: Sustained recovery management (UNODC, 2008) cites a case study of the people of the Alkali Lake Community in British Columbia, where alcohol dependence was having a serious effect on the tribal community. When some community members managed to stop drinking, including the chief of the reserve, a series of initiatives was undertaken including banning bootlegging, giving welfare money as food vouchers rather than cash, providing treatment rather than punishment for those involved in alcohol-related crimes, and creating a caring community environment. Fundamentally, an incentives and opportunities programme created economic enterprise and personal growth. The evidence suggests that this led to a huge increase in alcohol abstinence starting with less than 12 people and rising to 98% of the community, and that this change was accompanied by community improvements in family health, cultural activity and economic security. The report concludes that *'drawing on previously dormant social and spiritual capitals, in the form of returning to the teachings of their Native heritage, allowed the community in Alkali Lake to affect wellbriety'* (UNODC, 2008, p64).

Connecticut

In terms of wider systems, the next areas of focus are three US locations – Connecticut, Philadelphia and Chicago – where there have been systematic transitions to recovery approaches. The review will start with the work done in Connecticut. Kirk (2011) describes a process for facilitating sustained change at a worker and client programme and overall systems level towards a recovery model and the resulting improvements in core outcome indicators. Having established a set of core recovery values, the 'Promoting a recovery-oriented service system' policy was agreed in September 2002 to build on a strategic action plan developed in 2000. Central to the Connecticut model was identifying and applying tools for change, specifically:

■ a recovery self-assessment to be completed by service users, care staff and family members to assess commitment to recovery goals

■ a recovery institute – a tool for change on both the practitioner and systems based around the central model of an educational institute for recovery

■ an annual consumer satisfaction survey

■ a cross-state agency collaboration to assess change at a systems level.

As in the UK, the recovery model was threatened by local government deficits, yet the implementation of a Substance Abuse Treatment Enhancement Programme led to increases in activity and performance at no additional cost. These included a 24% reduction in re-admissions for detox, a 26% increase in residential rehabilitation admissions with no increase in bed capacity, and the initiation of a 24-hour call line. The process was based on repeated reviews to improve the overall plan, aggressive pursuit of external funding, and focusing on community life and natural supports. Built on a cycle of innovation, improved outcomes and reinvestment and savings, an intensive case management programme was developed that resulted in a 62% reduction in the use of acute services and a 14% reduction in the total treatment costs.

Connecticut was also home to the Connecticut Community for Addiction Recovery (CCAR), which involved the generation of recovery community centres (RCC) that acted as hubs for the delivery of a range of peer-based recovery support services (Valentine, 2011). The first RCC opened in 2004, with another three opening in the following two years. By 2009 the rate of activity was around 35,000 visits per year. The aim of the centres is to be a *recovery-oriented sanctuary anchored in the heart of the community* (Valentine, 2011, p266), as a central hub from which a range of peer services, primarily voluntary, can be run.

Addiction Recovery: A movement for social change and personal growth in the UK © Pavilion Publishing (Brighton) Ltd 2012

Each recovery community centre runs a core set of activities that includes:

- telephone recovery support – in the course of 2008, 276 volunteers contributed more than 13,000 hours to the service

- recovery employment services

- referrals to recovery housing

- re-engagement services for criminal justice clients

- a range of recovery groups

- training and education support

- family support

- volunteering and recovery coaching including peer one-to-one interactions.

Among the key principles Valentine concludes with are to listen to the people in recovery; that the culture of a recovery community is one of service and volunteering; to focus on the potential and not the pathology; and to *lead by example – expressions of love and kindness will foster an organisational culture of recovery and service*' (Valentine, 2011, p279).

Philadelphia

According to Achara-Abrahams *et al* (2011), the concept of recovery is becoming the prevailing paradigm in health policy in Philadelphia, based on three transformation components – changes in core values and principles, in practice and in regulations, funding and the community context. The model was based on starting with a powerful 'guiding coalition' who then took around six months to develop a recovery definition that worked locally and to establish a set of guiding principles. The next phase around the process was to communicate that vision and to ensure that stakeholders understood the nature of transformational change. Crucial to this process was the idea of 'early adopters' who enthusiastically embrace the recovery model and who were actively recruited to enable and support the process of organisational change.

The major practice changes that resulted were around:

- early engagement via outreach and community work

- strengths-based assessment processes and rapid access to services

■ focusing on retention in services with the client given more control and choice, and where the relationship was to be one of partnership or consultancy

■ the development of recovery-focused care services that were integrated with community groups and delivered in community settings

■ services are primarily peer-based and involve ongoing continuity of care through post-treatment check-ups and supports.

The model adopted involved identifying 'quick wins' and celebrating success, and links to local community strengths and resources, in this case including local faith organisations. Achara-Abrahams *et al* (2011) also argue that the effective transformation of the system relied on strong and informed leadership, but that leadership had to be closely allied to the communities and peer support systems.

Chicago

The Behavioural Health Recovery Management (BHRM) project established 11 principles of recovery over a four year period.

1. Maintain a recovery focus

2. Promote consumer empowerment with self-management

3. Support de-stigmatisation

4. Adopt evidence-based practice

5. Develop and apply clinical algorithms [protocols]

6. Utilise emerging technologies

7. Integrate addiction, mental health and primary care services

8. Establish recovery partnerships

9. Incorporate the ecology of recovery

10. Provide ongoing recovery and support

11. Promote ongoing evaluation

Another of the core challenges was to address cultural issues in each of the provider agencies and to address latent values, while also identifying and accessing viable funding sources. However, central to the approach was the

Recovery Coach Model and involving a training and support programme. This was a major programme of change and Boyle *et al* (2011) drew a number of key lessons from the transformation process:

- implementation is difficult and requires intensive ongoing supervision and the use of implementation fidelity measures

- it is critical to integrate with mental health and primary care services

- empowering is not the same as enabling, and the professional's job is to provide options, skills and help people overcome setbacks

- provide the services that are wanted by clients

- make sure that care plans are aligned with evidence-based practice

- develop core partnerships with funding bodies.

Overview of lessons from the US

The key conclusion from the US model is that implementing a recovery model takes time and considerable effort – the general consensus is that it takes between five and 10 years and that this change requires three levels of activity.

1. A strategic commitment and both leadership and planning.
2. Culture change and support for workers in specialist services and the active engagement of early adopters.
3. Engagement of local community resources and supports – including the development of recovery coaches and champions who work in the community enabling both early access to support and ongoing recovery support after the completion of formal treatment.

There are also issues around funding and sustainability that need to be part of the recovery vision and a mechanism for ensuring that change in addiction recovery systems is mapped against other forms of health provision – mental health and primary care – and linked to effective processes for engaging with training and employment agencies on the one hand, and housing support on the other. The latter two issues are also central to the 'community' concept and the idea that recovery models need to work with and build on what is already there in the community, not only specific to addiction recovery but also the pillars of community life that may include faith groups, community centres and service locations. But it is also likely to include at least one specialist hub that is iconic within the locality and has a role in supporting and developing champions and as a base for developing community engagement and peer activity.

The Lothians and Edinburgh Abstinence Programme and the model in Edinburgh

There have been a number of initiatives in Scotland that have attempted to build on indigenous recovery communities, but few of these have been located in the NHS. The Lothians and Edinburgh Abstinence Programme (LEAP) is a quasi-residential rehabilitation programme that is used as an example in the Scottish *Road to Recovery* drug strategy (Scottish Government, 2008). It is described there as '*deliver[ing] a recovery-orientated programme in the community by adapting activities and techniques often used in residential rehabilitation*' (Scottish Government, 2008, p25). There is a triangle of activity – a 12-step treatment programme delivered in the specialist centre, with links to supported housing where required and strong links to an intensive programme of vocational training and education. This is supplemented by a fourth element that is provided by the Serenity Café, which provides events and activities to promote recovery and offer social networks and supports.

In a special issue of the *Journal of Groups in Addiction and Recovery*, there are two articles about recovery in Edinburgh that enact the title of the issue 'Celebrating Recovery in the UK' – the first of these is about LEAP. McCartney (2011) described the key features of LEAP as:

- addressing the unmet medical needs of clients (based on a community detoxification programme)

- therapeutic activities based on group and individual counselling

- access to supported housing

- access to employment, training and education

- assertive linkage to mutual aid groups

- long-term aftercare

- structured activities and access to advice and support around nutrition and exercise.

LEAP operates as part of a partnership consisting of NHS Lothian's Substance Misuse Directorate, City of Edinburgh Council, Access to Industry and the Serenity Café. From this partnership, the service had a strong community recovery focus and a strong commitment to 12-step based interventions, resulting in almost 900 referrals in the first three years of its existence, resulting in 113 admissions per year (330 in total to date) with referrals primarily from general practice, specialist drug agencies and housing services. Of the first 103 admissions, 60% remained drug and alcohol free, and it is this group that spurred on the sense that LEAP had become a 'recovery hub' for a system change in Edinburgh. LEAP graduates have taken places on a number of national policy bodies – the National Forum on Drug Related Deaths in Scotland; the Drugs Strategy Delivery Commission; the Scottish Drugs Forum; the Scottish Drugs Recovery Consortium, as well as local commissioning and policy groups. In 2009, NHS Lothian opened up work placement opportunities for LEAP graduates to further increase the opportunities for workplace experience and links to 'mainstreaming' activity.

However, the key development for LEAP as a recovery hub has been its impact on the wider recovery community in Edinburgh. LEAP has an aftercare group that has developed a five-a-side football team, a guitar club, a recovery concert and a recovery chess league. But its relationship to the growth of mutual aid meetings in Edinburgh has been critical in its success. According to McCartney (2011), *'In 2006, the year before LEAP began treating patients, according to their respective websites, there were 10 mutual aid groups operating in Lothian aimed at supporting abstinence in drug misusers. Today [written in 2010] there are 22 meetings of Narcotics Anonymous (NA) and Cocaine Anonymous (CA) listed in the area'.*

While this cannot be causally attributed to the emergence of LEAP, there has been a dynamic sense of energy and growth in the recovery community in Edinburgh with LEAP (and in particular its aftercare group) acting as both the central hub and the 'shop window' for ongoing mutual aid and support. There are plans to develop SMART Recovery groups in the city with LEAP proposing to provide assertive linkage to such groups. There has also been some kind of knock-on effect in mainstream specialist services – from an initial opposition to mutual aid, there are now plans to roll out SMART groups across the city.

This energy and growth has also been enabled by the emergence of a second hub – the Serenity Café. In the same special issue of the *Journal of Groups in Addiction and Recovery* (JGAR), Campbell *et al* (2011) described the

Serenity Café as a social enterprise to provide a high street café-style social space that creates *"first step" employment, traineeships and volunteering opportunities for people in recovery trying to sustain abstinence'* (Campbell *et al,* 2011). The events, which are held monthly, not only provide a safe meeting and socialising space for people in recovery, but, through the development of a relationship with local treatment services, they provide access to recovery community contact for those still in treatment. This is an explicit operationalisation of 'social learning' exposure to recovery groups and champions where the attractiveness of recovery is made manifest to those earlier in their recovery journeys. The emerging activity has been of *'fortnightly, open-to-all planning meetings, with the further option for people to volunteer on the café-club night itself if this suits their need and availability'* (Campbell *et al,* 2011).

While the Serenity Café has also spawned a football team and a women's group, its central role is as a celebration of recovery that provides a visible social forum that is not affiliated to the 12-step fellowships, although many of those who attend the events are engaged with mutual aid groups. It is also quite clearly not 'treatment' but it plays a critical role in bringing together people at different stages of recovery and supporting their journeys. It is also critical as an emerging centre for collective recovery capital, and as a source of social learning and modelling of recovery (Moos, 2011). The services have continued to expand at LEAP with the addition in 2011 of a recovery drama group and a recovery choir, and also a recovery coach training programme.

But does this make Edinburgh a recovery-oriented system of care? In summarising where LEAP has got to, McCartney (2011) concludes that *'it may be challenging to further develop the LEAP model in terms of a roll out or even locally, although there are good reasons to look at doing precisely this'*, and this concern applies not only to the capacity and scale of the initiative but also its impact on the local system of care. Likewise, Campbell *et al* (2011) expressed their concerns about the funding and sustainability of the community development model and its impact on the 'mainstream' forms of provision. Although LEAP is located within the NHS, it is not clear at the time of writing whether it has become a core part of the mainstream system nor that this has developed to support or promote long-term recovery. There are some encouraging signs of LEAP acting as a conduit from structured treatment to both mutual aid and community organisations but less clear evidence that this has altered either the organisational structure of the care system nor the values or culture of many of those

Addiction Recovery: A movement for social change and personal growth in the UK ©
Pavilion Publishing (Brighton) Ltd 2012

working in the mainstream services. As a consequence, it seems that, at the time of writing, Edinburgh can more accurately be described as an emerging system driven by grassroots activity and a rapidly evolving mutual aid movement. It is the lack of bridges to recovery in treatment and the dominant pathology model in mainstream addiction treatment that would suggest that it is too early to characterise Edinburgh as a recovery-oriented system in spite of its very visible and dynamic recovery hubs.

Conclusion

There is a growing evidence base about recovery systems that is emerging to supplement our growing knowledge of individual pathways to recovery. The very existence of such an evidence base means that, despite the deeply personal nature of individual recovery, there are things that commissioners and service designers can do to augment recovery outcomes. The common themes from the US models are that this is a time-consuming process as it involves transformation at many levels – grassroots, service and system – that involve challenging and changing practices, beliefs and attitudes, and developing models and measures that reflect the values of recovery. There are also powerful shifts in where things happen (from the clinic to the community), who makes it happen (individuals in recovery with families and peers, in partnership with professionals whose role is significantly less central) and over what period of time (with emphasis on much longer periods of continuing support and care in peer-based settings and with appropriate attention paid to ongoing housing, training, vocational and social needs).

And there are real messages of hope – it can be a way of saving money, of accessing new funding sources and of generating hope in communities, but only if there is a real commitment to transformation and sustainable change. The process is more revolution than evolution and involves a localised vision of change that is communicated and facilitated through training, measurement and commitment to evaluating and implementing recovery-focused change. Although there are incredibly exciting initiatives in the UK – as exemplified by LEAP and the Serenity Café in Edinburgh – there is little clear evidence that this constitutes a recovery-oriented system. But the good news is that we need to add 'yet' to the end of this sentence and that the foundations are in place for recovery to become the dominant model – but only with the right level of strategic vision and bravery.

Key learning points

- Recovery is a philosophy that applies to treatment services and systems as well as to individuals.

- There are core underlying principles to a recovery system that are based on empowerment, choice and hope, that focus on strengths rather than pathologies.

- A recovery-oriented system involves a transition from the clinic to the community as the locus of intervention and from expert-patient to partnership as the basis for the therapeutic relationship.

- While there are early steps at recovery systems in the UK, there have been a number of successful transitions to recovery models in the US.

- This transition takes time and commitment and relies on a coalition of leaders, practitioners and members of local communities.

References

Achara-Abrahams I, Evans A & King J (2011) Recovery-focused behavioural health system transformation: A framework for change and lessons learned from Philadelphia. In: J Kelly & W White (Eds) *Addiction Recovery Management: Theory, research and practice*. Humana Springer: New York.

Babor T, Caulkins J, Edwards G, Fischer B, Foxcroft D, Humphreys K, Obot I, Rehm J, Reuter P, Room R, Rossow I & Strang J (2010) *Drug Policy and the Public Good*. Oxford University Press: Oxford.

Boyle M, Loveland D & George S (2011) Implementing recovery management in a treatment system. In: J Kelly & W White (Eds) *Addiction Recovery Management: Theory, research and practice*. Humana Springer: New York.

Campbell R, Duffy K, Gaughan M & Mochrie M (2011) The Serenity Café – on the road to recovery capital. *Journal of Groups in Addiction and Recovery* **6** (1–2) 132–163.

Centre for Substance Abuse Treatment (2009) *Guiding Principles and Elements of Recovery-Oriented Systems of Care: What do we know from the research?* Rockville, MD: Centre for Substance Abuse Treatment.

Finney J, Noyes C, Coutts A & Moos R (1998) Evaluating substance abuse treatment process models: Changes on proximal outcome variables during 12-step and cognitive behavioural treatment. *Journal of Studies on Alcohol* **59** 37–380.

Ilgen M, Tiet Q, Finney J & Moos R (2006a) Self-efficacy, therapeutic alliance, and alcohol-use disorder treatment outcomes. *Journal of Studies on Alcohol* **67** (3) 465–472.

Ilgen M, McKellar J, Moos R & Finney J (2006b) Therapeutic alliance and the relationship between motivation and treatment outcomes in patients with alcohol use disorder. *Journal of Substance Abuse Treatment* **31** (2) 157–162.

Kirk T (2011) Connecticut's journey to a state-wide recovery-oriented health-care system: Strategies, successes and challenges. In: J Kelly & W White (eds) *Addiction Recovery Management: Theory, research and practice*. Humana Springer: New York.

Klingemann H, Takala J & Humt G (1992) *Cure, Care or Control: Alcoholism treatment in sixteen countries*. Albany, NY: State University of New York Press.

McCartney D (2011) LEAP and the recovery community in Edinburgh, Journal of Groups in Addiction and Recovery. *Journal of Groups in Addiction and Recovery* **6** (1–2) 60–75.

Moos (2011) Processes that promote recovery from addictive disorders. In: J Kelly & W White (Eds) *Addiction Recovery Management: Theory, research and practice*. New York: Humana Press, Springer.

Scottish Government (2008) *The Road to Recovery: A new approach to tackling Scotland's drug problem*. Edinburgh: Scottish Government.

Smart R & Mann R (2000) The impact of programmes for high-risk drinkers on population levels of alcohol problems. *Addiction* **95** 37–52.

United Nations Office on Drugs and Crime (2008) *Drug Dependence Treatment: Sustained Recovery Management*. Available at: www.unodc.org/treatnet (accessed October 2011).

Valentine P (2011) Peer based recovery support services within a recovery community organisation: The CCAR experience. In: J Kelly & W White (Eds) *Addiction Recovery Management: Theory, research and practice*. Humana Springer: New York.

White W (2007) A recovery revolution in Philadelphia. *Counselor* **8** (5) 34–38.

Chapter 9

Strategic attempts to generate recovery-oriented systems of care in England: Recovery innovations in Yorkshire and Humberside

As a method of identifying, evaluating and promoting recovery initiatives, the National Treatment Agency for Substance Misuse's (NTA) regional office in Yorkshire and Humberside invited agencies and groups across the region to come forward with innovations at a service or a system level. These were then reviewed to assess how effective they were and what general rules could be identified about establishing recovery practice. The NTA regional office completed the initial short-listing and selected eight initiatives to be overviewed and evaluated by the author.

Two of the eight innovations focused on systemic changes in the drug action team areas of Barnsley and Calderdale, while the remaining six innovations were individual programmes. This chapter will focus on the attempts in Barnsley and Calderdale to generate recovery models in these funding and commissioning areas. It will focus on the initial stages of the attempts and the issues that arose in trying to engender commitment and buy-in across the two areas. The chapter will conclude with an overview of common themes and differences between the locations and some of the key implications for establishing a recovery-oriented system of care in the UK.

Barnsley

Until 2010, Barnsley's treatment system could be characterised as a system that was designed to provide rapid access to prescribing interventions. This was delivered through a mixed economy of GPs delivering treatment through a traditional 'shared care' model, a single GP/pharmacist 'primary care clinic', and central prescribing via the primary care trust. In addition, there was a local voluntary sector provider providing psychosocial interventions/structured day care, and two other third sector providers delivering low threshold interventions/young people's services and structured day care interventions. In terms of meeting national targets for drug treatment, this system was effective in terms of outputs, with low waiting times to access treatment and once clients were engaged in treatment, good retention – both targets established in the US recovery system models described in the previous chapter.

However, many service users felt that they were 'stuck' in the system. Once they entered treatment there was not much 'movement' within it – described as a 'silo system' – and organisations were working in isolation, working competitively and unwilling to refer people on and through the system. This ultimately resulted in poor outcomes. A decision was made by commissioners in 2009, following a comprehensive option appraisal, that the whole system should go out to open tender, with a view that 'recovery' should underpin the new system. A non-statutory provider successfully won the tender to manage the new process.

The successful partnership proposed a model based on a group of 'care navigators' who would sit independently of the treatment system to provide effective central assessment and recovery planning for each service user. The drive to implement the recovery approach has been driven centrally by the commissioning team using a top-down model based on a recognition of the limited recovery options available locally, the scarcity of mutual aid groups and the limited availability of access to community or residential detoxification or rehabilitation. In effect, Barnsley was trying to kick-start a recovery system as there was not a significant number of people already in recovery to act as peers, nor the recovery networks to support individuals and enhance the ability to maintain recovery.

Although it appears that Barnsley was attempting to kick-start recovery through commissioning, there is a growing recognition that this cannot happen overnight, and the recruitment of a recovery group – the Recovery Forum, which in turn transformed into the Barnsley Recovery Coalition – as well as involving housing and employment services was a recognition of both the scale and scope of the challenge. The author was also invited to be a consultant to the process and attempted to implement the Addiction Technology Transfer Centre model for implementing recovery approaches (ATTC, 2010). This consists of eight stages.

1. Establishing a great enough sense of urgency, and driving people out of their comfort zones.

2. Creating a sufficiently powerful guiding coalition who work together over time to effect change.

3. Creating a vision that sets the philosophy and direction of change.

4. Communicating that vision to all stakeholders consistently and regularly and generating buy-in.

5. Removing obstacles to the new vision, including worker attitudes and fears, and organisational structures and processes.

6. Systematically planning for and creating short-term wins to bolster confidence in the vision of change.

7. Not declaring victory too soon, and working with a plan for implementation that may take 5–10 years to complete.

8. Anchoring changes in the organisational culture.

It was felt that the re-commissioning process started the first stage of this process, but the recognition that it was ongoing and that the basic ideas about systemic change needed to be reinforced at regular intervals (Kelly & White, 2011). The focus of the initial endeavour was on points two to four of from the above list. The generation of a recovery coalition, engaging people in the development of a local recovery vision and then communicating that vision across the area. The actions that the emerging recovery champions engaged in were around raising recovery awareness in all key stakeholders in the area; creating a recovery coalition; establishing a vision for recovery and attempting to communicate that vision. These were set as the primary objectives for the first year of the system, along with addressing obstacles as they arose and attempting to generate some quick wins that would reinforce commitment to the coalition, and would create engagement and buy-in from wider professional groups.

Recovery training in Barnsley

The training days were held over seven days and just over 100 individuals attended. Attendees were primarily specialist drug and alcohol workers, but there were also service managers, peers, community group representatives and workers from link services, including housing, education and training, employment services and social care. The full-day session outlined the rationale for the recovery movement and policies and the implications for treatment, and provided workers with information on working in a recovery-oriented manner. At the end of each session, individuals were asked to volunteer to become 'champions' if they were willing to commit to leading and driving the process of recovery locally.

Recruiting champions

The initial meeting attempted to create three sub-groups.

1. **Strategic champions** – consisting largely of commissioners and managers who would attempt to clarify an organisational vision and model and consider the key challenges to be met in implementing recovery approaches.

2. **Therapeutic champions** – this group had as their primary aim changing the practices, attitudes and beliefs of specialist workers and assessing innovations to improve the recovery focus of treatment provision.

3. **Community champions** – this is the group of individuals (not just people in recovery but family members and others who are a part of the local community) whose task is to motivate and inspire recovery activity.

This model is consistent with the recovery champions model outlined in the English drug strategy (HM Government, 2010). It was important that it did not compartmentalise individuals so they were all asked to select the group that was most consistent with their interests, and participants were encouraged to change groups between sessions. Following introductions, participants were given the initial group task of identifying the core assets available to their group to realise a recovery vision – this approach is based on the concept of Asset Based Community Development (Kretzmann & McKnight, 1993). Kretzmann and McKnight (1993) argue that *'When practitioners begin with a focus on what communities have (their assets) as opposed to what they don't have (their needs) a community's efficacy in addressing its own needs increases, as does its capacity to lever in external support. It provides healthy community practitioners with a fresh perspective on building bridges with socially excluded people and marginalised groups'.*

This approach is useful in several respects; it encourages participants to think of their own community networks and how they might be mobilised; it taps into local civic pride; and it builds a map of a local community as a network of helping resources – some of them specific to addiction services and some more generic. It also encourages participants to think outside of the narrow specialist and professional services to non-specialised and non-professional community resources and community assets.

Establishing a vision

Having generated a map of shared community resources and those specific to strategic, service and community levels, each group then contributed to developing a vision of recovery for Barnsley. The overall vision was:

'Recovery is a reality that grows from within and is supported by peers and allies. To achieve this, our goal in Barnsley will be to create a community that supports individual and personal journeys in which we will minimize the obstacles and make no assumptions – only support their recovery. This should be led by a consortium of mixed groups with diverse skills and experiences working together as a recovery coalition for Barnsley.' (Barnsley Recovery Coalition, 2011)

The second session for the champions, who numbered around 30 and were primarily people in recovery but also workers from treatment services, commissioners and members of the local community, was about agreeing the overall strategy and working on ways of turning the vision into an implementation plan. It was also to identify communication mechanisms (for inside and beyond the champion group) and work out what 'quick wins' could be achieved (Kotter, 1996). In addition to email and telephone number exchanges it was agreed to set up a Barnsley Recovery Group on Facebook and to aim for some of the following core activities, split into the three sub-groups.

Strategic

- Stakeholder development events
- Opportunities to influence the overall treatment system and model
- Developing multiple pathways and options to recovery
- More effective linking in with employment and social enterprise

Therapeutic

- Changes in working practices to give workers more face-to-face time with clients
- Recovery-focused training run locally
- Unchaining workers to allow them to get out of the clinics and into communities

- Developing new processes for assessment and for client working

- Human resource models involving peers and based on recovery

Community

- More systematic involvement of arts and sports programmes

- Genuine menus of options for people attempting to access services

- A rolling programme of activities available to a wide range of people

- Creative writing classes

- Greater focus on peer mentoring

One of the arguments put forward against the idea of a 'recovery movement' is that it is nothing new and that people have been doing this kind of work for a long time (eg. Best *et al,* 2010). While it is true that people have been recovering for a long time, there are two primary mechanisms for recovery. The first is through 'mainstreaming' involving a new identity (frequently in a new location), which means the individual moves on with their lives and separates themselves from both the addict and the recovery community. The second is through mutual aid fellowships. While both options are essential parts of the recovery process for many, they do not generate a visible community of recovery.

The Coalition of Recovery Champions (CRC) approach allows a supportive and protective environment that enables individuals with different philosophies, and who may be at different stages of their own recovery, to come together with shared interests. It is likely that many of these individuals will also belong to mutual aid fellowships but the work in Barnsley demonstrates that it is possible to engage and support this kind of group strategically and to harness their considerable energies and enthusiasms. It remains to be seen what impact this will have on the delivery of the above recovery vision, but there is a strong commitment and sense of shared values and solidarity among the diverse CRC group in Barnsley to suggest that they will be able to deliver a range of community-level activities, to change practices and processes in formal treatment, and to create and deliver a model that will enable and support local recovery.

The final point to make in relation to the activity in Barnsley is about recovery leadership. There is a strong commitment from the drug action team to enabling a recovery vision but it is the strong, emerging community leadership that has provided real grounds for hope. There are emerging leaders from mutual aid, community development and diversionary activity backgrounds who will have the energy to enable the strategic vision by acting as visible icons of recovery success and shaping and driving a recovery strategy from a community base.

Calderdale

In contrast to Barnsley, Calderdale has had a growing recovery community for a number of years, initially driven forward by a therapeutic programme called Project Colt that focused on diversion to training and work, and for the last two years that was focused around the Basement Project, described in more detail below. At the time of writing, there were a number of recovery hubs in Calderdale:

- Basement Project (preparation for detox, champions, breakfast club, aftercare)
- Project Colt (training and employment)
- Freedom House (sober living housing)
- Connect 3 (community rehabilitation and linkage to housing and education and training services)
- Trust the Process (TTP) (agency offering a residential detoxification service in the neighbouring town of Bradford).

It is estimated that there are around 100 individuals actively involved in recovery projects, with less than 50 active in their recovery but not involved in services. According to a local needs assessment, at the end of 2008/09 around 700 individuals actively involved in either specialist treatment or engaged with treatment through primary care services in the area (Calderdale Drug Action Team, 2010). There were, however, only 51 problem drug users successfully discharged from treatment in 2009/10, and, as with the description of Edinburgh in Chapter 8, there is a concern that there is a recovery community that is poorly linked to the treatment system, and with poor rates of transition from treatment to any of the recovery groups mentioned.

In terms of the pathways to recovery, Calderdale Drug and Alcohol Partnership produced a guide to recovery called *Choices*, which attempts to support individuals through their recovery journey and help people to plan their recovery. The last section of the guide is a resources list that has contact details for three mutual aid groups (AA, NA, SMART), the three primary recovery services (Basement, Project Colt and Connect 3), the main treatment services (Calderdale Substance Misuse Services (SMS) and Alcohol service) and three other local services – the Women's Centre, Noah's Arc (counselling service) and Loved Ones United (family support).

What is innovative about Calderdale's recovery model?

The first point about the model used in Calderdale is that it offers an opportunity for individuals who are chaotic to access support without formal treatment. The Basement operates a breakfast café that is an open door access point, and contact with recovery champions who act as a bridge to the group programme and preparation for detoxification as well as routes to housing, training and family support. It provides a physical recovery hub in the centre of Halifax and a link to a wider array of recovery guides and mentors through links with the mutual aid fellowships.

What is particularly important about Calderdale is that the hubs are linked and supported through a particular kind of recovery champion – recovery leaders who provide a vision to shape a local recovery system. While the concept of 'recovery champions' is articulated in the UK Drug Strategy (HM Government, 2010), the strategy does not articulate how such champions may be connected or structured. What has emerged in Calderdale is the concept of indigenous recovery leadership but it is still at an early stage of development. While Calderdale does not have a large number of 'recovery elders' who are visible in the community or employed in the treatment services, there are key individuals in several of the recovery projects who have taken on a dynamic leadership role.

Calderdale remains an emerging recovery system because:

- there are clear philosophical differences about the nature and role of recovery between the specialist addiction services and the recovery projects and communities

- in particular, these crystallise around the role of 12-step fellowships and methadone maintenance prescribing

- there is no clear unitary vision for the area

- there are insufficient bridges between the treatment and the recovery communities

- there are pathways to recovery initiation but less clear pathways and recovery mentorship from recovery initiation to recovery maintenance

- the 'mainstreaming' option to stable housing, training, education and employment for those early in the recovery journey is relatively new and so not sufficiently established

- there are insufficient peer-led groups and activities that provide a diversity of recovery philosophies and rewarding activities, especially for individuals not engaged in the mutual aid fellowships.

At the time of writing, Calderdale is an innovative and dynamic emerging recovery community with strong community leadership and a rapid growth in recovery visibility and impact on the local community. However, this leadership is clustered in a small number of individuals who are outside of the specialist treatment system and whose approach and philosophy is seen as a threat by some provider agencies. There is also a speed of change issue. While the emerging recovery organisations are dynamic and rapidly evolving, this poses a threat in two respects. First, there is insufficient opportunity for the peers and volunteers to develop the experience and the skills to occupy the increasingly diverse and professional roles required of them. Second, this places a strain on the system in that both the structures of commissioning and specialist provision (particularly clinical provision) are not able or willing to change at an equivalent pace, and so there is a real demand on the commissioners to develop a clear strategy and vision for recovery implementation that will enable and support the differential rates of practice and culture change.

Part of this process is around community recovery leadership and 'succession planning'. One of the most challenging aspects of developing visible recovery communities is around building up active engagement in 'graduates' who move on with their lives and, for at least a period of time, want to detach themselves from the active using and early recovery populations. Some of them will do this by geographic separation (Best *et al,* 2009) and others by a change in identity (McIntosh & McKegany, 2001) that precludes ongoing involvement in recovery communities. The challenge in places like Calderdale is to create the 'behavioural economics' that makes ongoing engagement in recovery communities attractive and valuable as part of both moving on with mainstream aspects of life and with their own recovery journey (Moos, 2011). In Calderdale, this has taken the form of emerging recovery hubs that are physically located in the town of Halifax and the prominence and dynamism of several key individuals. However, their efforts are only sustainable if each cohort of programme graduates includes one or two individuals who are inspired and motivated to continue their own recovery journey by modelling and learning from visible champions and becoming part of that energy and shared purpose. In Calderdale, the recovery community has reached a critical crossroads where the capacity of a small number of visible champions is being stretched and the support of specialist services, commissioners and their own recovery networks will be essential in ensuring that the recovery community continues to develop and flourish.

Conclusion

Barnsley and Calderdale are at different stages in the growth of recovery communities and their impact on the local communities. The situation described in Barnsley is an example of what White (2008) referred to as the 'swamping' of the recovery community by the effectiveness and success of the treatment system. In meeting government targets around numbers in treatment and retention, Barnsley had created a highly effective engagement and retention treatment model in which most clients were effectively stabilised and their lives normalised but with very little movement towards either abstinence or towards wider recovery objectives. In Barnsley, the inspiration and success has been around both changing professional cultures and developing a recovery coalition involving professionals and community champions from an impressive diversity of backgrounds and recovery philosophies.

In contrast, the recovery system in Calderdale has been emerging for around two years and there are both physical recovery hubs, abstinence-oriented services and a network of visible recovery champions. There still remain tensions over the transition to system-wide recovery principles and processes and there is not a clear and consistent vision for recovery. This has resulted in capacity issues both in terms of the number of people who are able to move from treatment services to recovery communities and the capacity of the recovery services to initiate and particularly to sustain their recovery journeys. This is a practical issue of switching to recovery systems – it is much easier and cheaper to treat lots of clients in outpatient opiate substitution programmes than in specialist recovery groups, which may have limited capacity for both detoxification and for programmes. The second problem is more complex and involves human and interpersonal factors in developing networks of champions with shared values and a commitment to sustaining recovery endeavours in a more diverse array of community activities and settings. In Chapter 10, the focus will switch to two locations with longer established recovery communities – Liverpool and the Wirral – to try to identify the structure and system of 'mature' recovery communities in the UK.

Key learning points

- There is a number of exciting and innovative programmes of recovery underway in the UK, two of which have been highlighted.

- In Barnsley, the model was based on an awareness-raising programme that recruited recovery champions who met to develop a strategy and to work together with the commissioners.

- In Calderdale, the model was based on a grassroots movement of change based on early engagement and community support.

- In both places, there were organisational and cultural barriers but the commitment of participants generated a movement towards coalition and mutual support.

References

Addiction Technology Transfer Centre (2010) *Recovery-Oriented Systems of Care: Training of facilitators manual.* Kansas City, MO: Addiction Technology Transfer Center (ATTC) National Office.

Barnsley Recovery Coalition (2011) *Barnsley Recovery Treatment System Newsletter.* Barnsley: Barnsley Drug and Alcohol Action Team.

Best D, Day E, Morgan B, Oza T, Copello A & Gossop M (2009) What treatment means in practice: An analysis of the therapeutic activity provided in criminal justice drug treatment services in Birmingham, England. *Addiction Research and Theory* **17** (6) 678–687.

Best D, Bamber S, Battersby A, Gilman M, Groshkova T, Honor S, McCartney D & Yates R (2010) Recovery and straw men: An analysis of the objections raised to the transition to a recovery model in UK addiction services. *Journal of Groups in Addiction and Recovery* **6** (5) 264–288.

Calderdale Drug Action Team (2010) *Business and Recovery Plan.* Personal communication.

HM Government (2010) *Drug Strategy 2010: Reducing demand, restricting supply, building recovery: Supporting people to live a drug-free life.* London: Home Office.

Kelly J & White W (2011) *Addiction Recovery Management: Theory, research and practice.* New York: Humana Press: Springer.

Kotter J (1996) *Leading Change.* Massachusetts: Harvard Business School Press.

Kretzmann J & McKnight J (1993) *Building Communities from the Inside Out: A path towards finding and mobilising a community's assets.* Evanston, IL. ABCD Institute.

McIntosh J & McKeganey N (2001) *Beating the Dragon: The recovery from dependent drug use.* London: Prentice Hall.

Moos R (2011) Processes that promote recovery from addictive disorders. In: J Kelly & W White (Eds) *Addiction Recovery Management: Theory, research and practice.* New York: Springer-Science.

White W (2008) *Recovery Management and Recovery-Oriented Systems of Care: Scientific rationale and promising practices.* Pittsburgh, PA: Northeast Addiction Technology Transfer Center, Great Lakes Addiction Technology Transfer Center, Philadelphia Department of Behavioural Health and Mental Retardation Services.

Chapter 10

An analysis of 'mature' recovery systems in England

This chapter follows on from Chapter 9 by examining two further recovery systems, in Liverpool and the Wirral. Along with Calderdale (see Chapter 9), the author formally reviewed Liverpool and the Wirral as recovery innovation sites as part of a broader policy initiative sponsored by the National Treatment Agency (NTA) in England. The first section of the chapter explains the background and rationale for the initiative and gives an overview of the treatment and recovery systems in each area. An overview of the clients' experiences of recovery in each area is summarised, before a comparison and synthesis of recovery models and approaches is given. Finally, it reviews the implications of this synthesis to answer the following questions:

- Can Liverpool or the Wirral be described as a recovery-oriented system of care?

- What is the role of providers and commissioners in enabling the growth of recovery communities and recovery systems?

Recovery-oriented drug treatment and segmentation

In 2010, the NTA convened an expert group of clinicians and other interested parties to assess the principles of open-ended opiate substitute prescribing with a view to developing guidance focusing on abstinence and long-term recovery. It also aimed to develop patient placement criteria that would assess individual drug users and decide which treatment service model would be of most benefit. In relation to this second goal, the author was commissioned to come up with a method for segmenting the treatment and non-treatment populations based on their likelihood of achieving meaningful recovery. This latter task was overseen by a sub-group of experts from the field, and was to be based on a rapid assessment method.

The method selected mirrored a previous priority review the author was involved in during 2005 for the Prime Minister's Delivery Unit (PMDU) on the effectiveness of drug treatment (the report was a restricted government document). The method was based on the selection of three test sites and the central collation of information about these sites before additional data was gathered on week-long site visits and tested against local data sources and local expert knowledge. For the review of Liverpool, the Wirral and Calderdale, the starting point was the conceptual model of recovery outlined in Chapter 4, to be supplemented by centrally held data on the treatment population in the three test sites, and data to be collected from people in recovery and providers of services in each location.

The sites selected were a 'mature' recovery community (Liverpool), an integrated recovery system (the Wirral) and an emerging recovery community (Calderdale, as outlined in Chapter 9). While the focus of the chapter will be on each of the participating sites' – and particularly on their recovery system – it is worth giving an overview of the basic model and results.

The central data analysis was conducted using two types of data held centrally as part of a data monitoring system – the National Drug Treatment Monitoring System (NDTMS), a data source about numbers accessing treatment, and the Treatment Outcome Profile (TOP), a short assessment of functioning completed at treatment intake and at subsequent three-month reviews. The latter was central to assessing recovery functioning in the current analysis. The models that were tested using the data available from this source were:

- the existence of basic 'enablers' of recovery using the Rethink (2008) model, which suggests that before it is possible to start on a recovery journey, an individual must have some basic human rights and choices, a safe place to live that is free from threat and be free from acute physical and psychological symptoms

- recovery as a developmental process that emerges over time and the trajectory of change in and beyond treatment is indicative of the recovery progress

- the idea of recovery capital at the heart of change (Granfield & Cloud, 2001), and that, as individuals develop the personal and social resources, there will be measurable and demonstrable change in recovery capital

- changes at an individual level are underpinned by aspects of collective recovery capital

(Best & Laudet, 2010).

The initial analysis examined the basic recovery capital factors, which were operationalised as:

- abstinence from the use of crack cocaine and heroin

- no acute housing problems reported

- a form of structured activity (operationalised as at least one day of employment, training or formal education in the last month).

Although there was some variation between sites, this was not marked and, regardless of time in treatment and location, more than 80% of clients in structured drug treatment in the community reported no housing problems, just under half reported abstinence from both heroin and cocaine in the last month, and around 10–15% were engaged in some form of structured activity. However, when the proportion that had achieved all three recovery enablers was assessed, the overall average for the treatment populations in the three locations was around eight per cent, irrespective of time in treatment. There was no discernible improvement over time, and in effect, only one in 12 individuals in the three participating sites would qualify as ready for their recovery journeys. There is little indication that this factor improves with time in treatment – the groups studied represented those in the early months of treatment, those engaged for 6–12 months, for one to three years and those in treatment for more than three years. It is important to note that the data is cross-sectional and does not represent change over time in the same people – it is a snapshot of treatment populations in 2009–2010.

The Treatment Outcome Profile (TOP) form (Marsden *et al*, 2008) also assesses three aspects of subjective well-being – physical health, psychological health and quality of life – with participants asked to rate these on a scale ranging from 0–20 (see Table 10.1). The ratings were then used to create a subjective measure of recovery to supplement the 'hard' markers of enabling life circumstances. Encouragingly, there were strong and consistent relationships between the number of recovery enabling factors that clients in structured drug treatment reported, and their well-being. The more enablers a person had the better the quality of life they reported, irrespective of whether they were new to treatment or had been in treatment for a long period of time. From this initial calculation, the first model that was developed is that the basis for a recovery capital measure is a combination of objective and subjective indicators, some of which are at least partly captured with the basic treatment monitoring measures used in England.

Table 10.1: Basic map of recovery indicators available from the TOP form

Objective	Stable accommodation
	No reported use of heroin and cocaine
	Some level of employment or training
Subjective	Physical health
	Psychological health
	Quality of life

To create an overall scale, for each of the 'objective enablers' present a score of 1 was given and 0 if it was absent. For the 'subjective' measures of well-being, the scales are scored between 0–20 by participants and this was recoded to a score of between 0 and 1 – in this way both scales had a range of 0–3 and so an overall recovery score of 0–6 could be created. The process of growth in subjective well-being is not linear, with the gains reported typically peaking at a relatively early stage of treatment. Consistent with treatment outcome literature, the subjective sense of well-being for a treatment population peaks at between 6–12 months into treatment and then starts to tail off. In all three of the pilot sites, the average score peaks (at just under two out of 6) for clients between six months and one year into treatment, and then starts to decline. Across the three sites, the average recovery capital score is much higher at six months than at treatment entry, grows slightly towards the end of the first year in treatment, and then starts to decline.

In attempting to assess what this change means in terms of recovery capital, changes in recovery capital from baseline to six months for the three different measures – objective enablers, subjective recovery and overall recovery – were then charted. For the objective model, only which Drug Action Team people were living in was significant, while for both the subjective and the objective the only significant factor in the regression was whether the client was an opiate addict. In other words, as is consistent with the published treatment outcome literature, opiate addicts show the most clear improvement (in this case in recovery factors and well-being) from the baseline to follow-up (odds ratio = 2.59).

The next analysis of the NTA data attempted to assess the relationship between recovery capital factors and treatment outcomes, using the only outcome variable available using the limited structured data available to this analysis, which was 'discharge reason'. For those who had planned discharges from treatment (which typically means a successful completion of the treatment episode), the mean recovery capital score was just over 3 out of 6, with markedly lower average scores for both the unplanned discharge group (those dropping out or discharged for disciplinary infractions) and those retained in treatment.

Those who ended up having a planned discharge from treatment had an average baseline recovery capital score of 3; those with unplanned discharges had baseline recovery capital scores of 2.7; those transferred had baseline capital scores of 2.8 and an average score of 2.8 was also recorded for those retained in treatment. In other words, there is no clear evidence that the long-term retained group are either 'low functioning and chaotic' or a 'high functioning' group. When this analysis was repeated, but using the TOP recovery capital scores from the most recent review rather than from the baseline, a similar picture emerges. Those who have planned discharges have the highest recovery capital at their most recent review point (mean = 3.9), compared to a mean of 3.1 for those with unplanned discharges and 3.2 for those who are transferred to other services. The difference between the recovery capital scores of the planned and the other three groups is significant in Tukey's post-hoc tests. In other words, people who have a positive treatment outcome reported significantly better overall recovery capital than those still in treatment or with less positive reasons for discharge.

While this is not a complete justification or vindication of the summary method from the monitoring data collected on TOP, it suggests that both objective recovery enablers and subjective experiences of well-being represent viable and consistent markers of progress to be tested in more detailed analysis of personal recovery journeys.

Developing the model testing with personal recovery stories

In the second phase of the development of the recovery model, the monitoring data from TOP was further tested by structured data collecting visits to the three pilot sites. The purpose of the visits was:

- to map the recovery communities and their relationships to the treatment systems

- to map the recovery functioning of the visible recovery communities

- to test the TOP-based model with more in-depth research analysis of recovery capital and recovery functioning.

The research team spent a week in each of the three locations and four field interviewers had the challenge of attempting to access and recruit the 'visible recovery community'. The assumption is that the entire recovery community is not accessible as a consequence of natural recovery, 'mainstreaming' and anonymous recovery through the mutual aid fellowships. In each of the areas there will be people who have achieved recovery independently and without any form of mutual aid engagement as well as those whose lives have moved on and are not accessible or willing to participate in recovery research. For this reason, the project aimed to access and recruit a visible recovery community consisting of those with some contact with either mutual aid groups or recovery support groups, and who were willing to tell their recovery stories. This was in part a test of recovery networks but it was primarily a test of the recovery communities who would be available as social icons (Moos, 2011) and mentors for people engaged in recovery processes.

In total, 176 visible recovery champions were recruited between the three sites, including 80 recovery champions from Liverpool and 47 from the Wirral. Before moving onto the specific recovery stories in these locations, an overview will be provided of the themes of recovery common to this group. 31.7% were in recovery from drugs only, 42.7% from drugs and alcohol, and 25.6% from alcohol only. On average, the participants reported that they were in recovery for a mean of 40.4 months (range from less than one month to 23 years). The mean age of the sample was 41.5 years (±9.1), with the sample ranging in age from 19 to 69 years. This group was slightly older on average than the typical population in treatment, which will typically access treatment in their early 30s. The fundamentally social contagion of recovery is evident in the finding that 114 participants reported that they had encouraged other people to attend at least one recovery group in the last month – this totalled 1,223 individuals who had been encouraged to attend by people participating in the project.

While around eight per cent of the treatment population from monitoring data reported all three of the objective recovery enablers, the comparable figure for the active recovery group was 44.9%. For the two locations, the split is dramatic:

- Liverpool – 41.3% (in treatment – 4%)
- Wirral – 55.3% (in treatment – 6%)

There are some critical relationships that were identified for the recovery population:

- the longer someone is in recovery, the more enablers they report (r=0.18, p<0.05)

- there are consistent positive correlations between how many of the three enablers people in recovery report and their physical well-being (r=0.18, p<0.05), psychological well-being (r=0.32, p<0.001) and quality of life(r=0.17, p<0.05)

- there are clear relationships between well-being and activity (training or employment):
  - activities in last month and physical health (r=0.28, p<0.01)
  - activities in last month and psychological health (r=0.44, p<0.001)
  - activities in last month and overall quality of life (r=0.29, p<0.001).

As with the regressions for the overall treatment population in the three sites, engaging in structured activity is consistently identified as a positive predictor of recovery functioning. Thus, while time in recovery matters, as has been shown in previous UK addiction research (Hibbert & Best, 2011), the current findings would suggest that this effect is mediated by what people do. In other words, duration of recovery may only lead to improvements in quality of life and well-being if that time has been spent actively engaging in meaningful activities.

Testing the basic recovery model with more in-depth indicators

The three recovery measures that were also collected to assess against the TOP-based recovery summary were the Recovery Group Participation Scale (Groshkova, *et al,* 2011) and two elements of the Assessment of Recovery Capital (Groshkova *et al,* submitted) – personal recovery capital and social recovery capital. Basic scores on each of these indicators are reported in Table 10.2.

Table 10.2: Data reported on recovery scales

SCALE	SCORING	Mean, SD	Range
Recovery Group Participation Scale (RGPS)	0–14, higher scores meaning greater engagement in recovery groups	10.1 (±3.8)	0–14
Assessment of Recovery Capital (ARC) – personal	0–25, higher scores meaning greater personal recovery capital	21.4 (±3.9)	8–25
Assessment of Recovery Capital (ARC) – social	0–25, greater scores meaning greater social recovery capital	20.7 (±4.4)	6–25

The comparison between scores on each of these factors and the data collected on TOP-based recovery measures are given in Table 10.3.

Table 10.3: Links between TOP-related recovery indicators and more focused measures of recovery well-being

	Objective recovery scores (0–3)	Subjective recovery scores (0–3)	Total recovery scores (0–6)
RGPS	0.05	0.17*	0.13
ARC – personal	0.19*	0.45***	0.39***
ARC – social	0.19*	0.38***	0.34***
Days of activity	0.70***	0.27**	0.63***
Time in recovery	0.18*	-0.08	0.05

In other words, there were good relationships between subjective recovery and measures of recovery capital, but these relationships were weaker for the objective indicators of recovery.

The study also attempted to assess social networks in a more systematic way than done previously. To do this, the Royal Society of the Arts (RSA) was recruited to provide assistance and the format was used in the Connected Communities work (RSA, 2010), but abridged to suit the current project aims. This involved asking participants to provide names of people in their social networks – something not typically done in addiction research. This provoked some anxiety among the research team and the managers of services, and so participants were told not to answer the question if they felt uncomfortable. Nonetheless, 163 of 176 participants provided either a first name, a designation (eg. parent, girlfriend) or initials for at least one person.

Across the sample of 176 participants, a total of 610 important individuals were named to the researchers, of whom 21 were active users, 264 were in recovery and 310 were non-users. On average, the number of close friends reported was 3.4, of whom 1.5 were in recovery on average. The number of people in the social network reported correlated with personal ($r=0.27$, $p<0.001$) and social ($r=0.31$, $p<0.001$) recovery capital, and the number in recovery in the social network also correlated, but not as strongly with both personal ($r=0.17$, $p<0.05$) and social ($r=0.19$, $p<0.05$) recovery capital. In other words, there are important aspects of recovery that are immersed in the social networks of individuals – both who they spend time with and how many of these close friends there are.

In terms of developing an overall model of recovery, this contributes to a dynamic model of recovery likelihood that is based primarily on the personal and social resources that the individual has. However, even if social networks are strong and constitute closed communities, there remain broader elements of the lived community that can impact on the likelihood of recovery success. In the three pilot sites, three of these factors were given particular prominence.

1. The accessibility and quality of treatment services and the extent to which specialist treatment providers were linked to community recovery groups and mutual aid societies.

2. The attractiveness, scale, scope and diversity of recovery groups and recovery champions in the local area.

3. The level of opportunity for sober living housing and for education, training and employment opportunities in each area, along with overall community markers for community cohesion and well-being.

The analysis of Liverpool and the Wirral describes two further case studies of transition to recovery communities and an overall overview of the relationship between recovery communities and personal recovery journeys follows.

Liverpool: A dynamic and evolving recovery community

The research team was able to access and interview 80 individuals who were visible and enthusiastic in the recovery community over three days. The reason this was possible is because Liverpool has a number of established powerful and dynamic recovery hubs and the team had support from specialist treatment agencies that are beginning to embrace a recovery agenda. There are two primary recovery hubs – The Parkview Project and Genie in the Gutter – which are rehabilitation services for alcohol and drug users that provide intensive, ongoing support but also, crucially, act as a bridge between formal treatment provision and mutual aid and other community groups. Both take referrals and admissions from mainstream health addiction treatment providers and successfully link these clients into a wide range of community groups, including 12-step and other mutual aid provision.

The Parkview Project is a two-stage residential rehabilitation service in the heart of Liverpool that is linked to both an emerging alumni association (PACT) and to a well-established community recovery support organisation – Genie in the Gutter. Genie in the Gutter is unique in providing a community in the heart of the city that is available to individuals (prescribed and abstinent) who are in the early stage of their recovery journey. The key providers of recovery-oriented support, which act as bridges between specialist treatment and the non-professional recovery community, are as follows:

- The Self-Help Addiction Recovery Programme (SHARP) is an intensive 12-step community rehabilitation service that operates over a 12-week programme and has a weekly aftercare programme. SHARP is also currently planning a recovery café for the city.

- Additionally, there are other key components of a recovery system, including a recovery-focused homeless centre, the Basement, which provides support and education, as well as access to detoxification, and is strongly linked to the specialist recovery services.

- The Spider Project provides training and diversionary activities for people further along their recovery journeys.

- The Independence Project offers limited inpatient detoxification but primarily runs an education and training programme that aims to 'mainstream' clients as quickly as possible towards effective reintegration into their own communities.

Addiction Recovery: A movement for social change and personal growth in the UK ©
Pavilion Publishing (Brighton) Ltd 2012

■ In addition, one of the two specialist treatment providers, Addaction, has developed increasing links with the recovery communities and jointly runs recovery workshops.

■ At the time of writing, Liverpool had the fastest growing network of mutual aid meetings in Europe.

The estimates derived for the size of the visible recovery population (excluding those who attend only the anonymous fellowships) was 300 (with a range of 250–350), with many individuals making use of several of the recovery organisations listed above. In contrast, it is estimated that there are around 3,000 clients who attend the two specialist treatment providers – Addaction and Mersey Care – with senior managers at Mersey Care, the primary NHS treatment service, acknowledging that there were low levels of stable recovery in their active clients and little transition from specialist treatment to recovery communities. Within the range of NHS services, there is a specialist inpatient detoxification unit, the Kevin White Unit, with a capacity for 17 beds, although only 15 of these are commissioned at present. The duration of stay is between seven and 28 days, with 70% of the beds typically used for detoxification and 30% for stabilisation. However, the service management estimated that 80% of admissions were re-admissions. This is a major indicator of effectiveness not only for recovery initiation but also a marker for the overall effectiveness of the recovery system.

In 2010, the NTA published data that suggested that 36% of completions of treatment of problem drug users do not re-appear in either custody or treatment, potentially constituting a target outcome rate for completion successes. Thus, if the primary enabling treatment for starting recovery has a re-admission rate of 80%, it would suggest that either the wrong people are accessing the detoxification service or that there are inadequate pathways to recovery support for completions.

The perception that the main treatment services were mired in a harm reduction philosophy was supported by a senior manager from Mersey Care, who asserted that: *'The recovery agenda has been bubbling for a couple of years – under a different name but Mersey Care were slow in adopting it. We have been stuck in the harm reduction movement. We are slowly integrating recovery – and begun to improve this transparently'* (Merseycare manager, personal communication). This has included developing links with Intuitive Recovery and with SMART Recovery, and the perception that there is a small number of people in medicated recovery and that Mersey Care is actively trying to change culture about moving people on – service user change and staff change. However, there was the perception that around a third of the staff in Mersey Care were actively resistant to the recovery agenda, and that there was considerably more work to do. Within Mersey Care, there is the perception that progress is being made and that increased joint working is taking place not only with partner agencies like Jobcentre Plus, but also with SHARP whose recovery advocates are engaging Mersey Care clients in their reception area.

The second mainstream treatment provider is Addaction. There are four main elements to their provision – young people, criminal justice, shared care and community services that include service user development work, links to SMART and 12-step fellowships, and links to employment services, family workshops and recovery workshops. Addaction is more established as a 'bridge' service, creating multiple routes and pathways to recovery support and encouraging direct contact with recovery services both at Addaction premises and through workshops linking to the main recovery communities in Liverpool.

However, Liverpool remains a primarily 'split' system with a vibrant recovery community that is well supported and resourced that has only limited links to the two large treatment providers. Although there is some evidence that both Mersey Care and Addaction are continuing to make changes in their systems, the speed of transition is slow, and there are ongoing cultural issues about the extent of the transition to a recovery-oriented approach. Furthermore, the system remains primarily a 'treatment system' with recovery as a stage alongside and beyond treatment. There is no clear and coherent recovery vision for this system, and the evolution of recovery in Liverpool will require a significant shift in attitudes (which are frequently polarised), systems which are treatment-heavy, and effective bridging mechanisms between recovery and treatment models. Thus, while Liverpool has impressive and visible hubs and champions of recovery, there is still more indication that it has a treatment system based on an acute care model, rather than a recovery system based on effective bridging and rapid engagement with recovery communities.

The Wirral: the emergence of a recovery model

According to the 2008/09 Wirral Drug Action Team's annual report (Wirral Drug Action Team, 2009), 2,883 people accessed drug treatment services in 2007/08, with 88% achieving 12-week retention.

Services: There are around 1,600 people in treatment – about 850 in the shared care and recovery team – who should be the most stable clients and are typically on low dose prescriptions. Of this group, about 180 clients are actively involved in detoxification; in other parts of the service, others are in slow reduction programmes, although there is a recognition that the change process is a slow one. However, there is a key post within the Wirral Drug Services (WDS) – that of a 'recovery navigator' whose job it is to enable movement to recovery services and to raise awareness among treatment clients about the possibility of recovery. Within the main provider agency there is also a cohort of active recovery champions who have acted as both 'personal bridges' and as key agents of culture change, although the estimate from senior managers was that there is still a group of around a third of workers who are resistant to recovery activities. There is also a strong service user group called Inner Action and the Service Users' Recovery Forum (SURF).

There are additional services run by ARCH Initiatives, a non-governmental organisation providing community and criminal justices' addiction services, and by Trust the Process (TTP). The structured day care programme run by ARCH accepts referrals from either the inpatient detoxification service or from Phoenix Futures and is for abstinent clients. The programme consists of 24 weeks of contact – in the first 12 weeks clients receive psychosocial interventions, life skills, motivational interviewing, transactional analysis, and in the next 12 weeks there is more focus on education – skills training, IT and creative arts. At the second stage there is less focus on daily attendance; the expectation is that people are engaged with 'move on' services like the Spider Project and the voluntary service. As with most of the Wirral services there is a vibrant service user group at ARCH that typically attracts 10–20 people. The ARCH aftercare centre also acts as a physical recovery hub and a part of a recovery network that is also linked to the local Methodist church where 12-step meetings are held.

TTP provides psychosocial interventions based on the 12-step recovery model and provides community support and recovery group process. It also provides an active outreach service through criminal justice and the

YMCA. Phoenix Futures offers both a residential rehabilitation service with a bed capacity of 32 and a planned stay of six months. While clients do not all originally come from the Wirral, many will continue to live in the local community on completion of their residential stay. Crucial to the programme is the re-entry service involving local housing with floating support and links to a range of community projects including ARCH aftercare, the Spider Project, the Independence Initiative and to 12-step fellowships, where appropriate. There is increasing commitment to volunteering and community engagement and Phoenix Futures also actively engages in a range of social enterprises.

Communities of recovery: There are two main recovery communities – those that originate in the residential rehabilitation service provided by Phoenix Futures and those that have grown up around the 12-step fellowships (with considerable overlap with the mutual aid movement in Liverpool). There are seven AA, six NA and one CA meeting every week in the Wirral, and a diverse range of recovery activities run by Wirral Community Voluntary Services (CVS), the Spider Project, by Social Partnership and in partnership with a number of the providers. Social Partnership in particular, as a community-based service, provides an alternative for people who do not want to attend treatment services.

There is estimated to be around 10 community recovery champions linked to the formal treatment services and a further 10 outside the treatment network in the Wirral. There is also a diverse range of recovery activities including:

- a recovery fishing club
- a boxing club
- a cycling group
- a conservation project
- SMART recovery.

The Wirral also offers access to the Independence Project in Liverpool and to Intuitive Recovery for those who want to and are able to rapidly access 'mainstreaming' opportunities.

Systems: Within the Wirral, there is a high level of commitment to recovery, and the emergence of an integrated system based on a diverse array of champions. A recovery event was held in New Brighton in December 2010 and had more than 500 professionals and people in recovery in attendance. The Drug Action Team has developed a recovery systems model that attempts to performance-manage around recovery goals and objectives. There are indications of positive linkage between NHS treatment, ongoing professional supports and community activities.

There are ongoing systems issues around the role of 12-step – particularly challenging for the traditional philosophies of Wirral Drug Services (with a commitment to a harm reduction model) and Phoenix Futures (with a therapeutic community model). The Wirral Drug Action Team has developed a proactive recovery model that is designed to empower *'drug and alcohol users to make positive changes, achieve abstinence and leave treatment on a longer lasting road to recovery – completely free of drugs and / or alcohol'* (Wirral Drug Action Team, 2011).

There remains a problem for the Wirral in terms of establishing a clear strategy for change that is coherent across the system and that will enable a speed of change that is consistent for both statutory treatment providers and an emerging recovery community. There is a clear indication that recovery is effectively being embedded as a principle for working across specialist community services and that this is influencing community activities, but the speed of transition is inconsistent across providers with many clients continuing to be 'stuck' on long-term opiate substitution prescriptions.

The Wirral has very effectively created 'agents of change' within the specialist prescribing service and allowed recovery contagion to emerge from attractive and visible champions accessing a range of 'stuck' clients. To support this initial engagement with recovery, there are emerging bridges to both a diverse range of recovery hubs and philosophies across the area, that are both localised through Social Partnership, and spread across professionally facilitated groups and projects (such as ARCH café and aftercare) and exclusively peer activities (the sports programmes and mutual aid groups). The final key strength that the Wirral has is a dynamic commissioning model that provides rapid responses to service gaps and which is committed to a vision of an integrated recovery system. The next phase of this transition will be to operationalise this vision and translate it into the type of action plan that has been specified in the work of Achara-Abrahams *et al* (2011).

While the Wirral is closest to a coherent recovery system, it lacks what is needed nationally, which is a measurement system that allows and enables effective measurement of recovery at:

■ individual client level

■ family level

■ worker and service level

■ system level

■ community level.

The development of this 'performance management' model is needed alongside the decision to establish and then commit to a vision for recovery that is linked to an implementation plan that can be 'sold' to key stakeholders, recovery champions and the wider community. The iteration of this vision will be the basis for establishing localised UK recovery models.

What are the lessons from Liverpool and the Wirral?

In both areas there are real grounds for optimism about the establishment of recovery-oriented systems, although both have different profiles of strengths and each is currently in a different place. In Liverpool, there is an extremely strong and well-established visible recovery community based on key champions and central hubs that generate visible recovery contagion. Yet there is little evidence that the overall treatment system has evolved sufficiently to maximise these benefits. There is also a slowly changing treatment system that is around 10 times as large as the visible recovery community that exists for many clients in isolation of the recovery communities, and there is still a polarised separation of recovery and treatment. This is not the case in the Wirral where the bridges to recovery are much stronger, where treatment services accommodate both bridges and community champions, and where there is a greater sense of cohesion in recovery approaches.

However, both recovery systems are fragile. Each relies heavily on a small number of personalities to continue the push from a 'treatment' model based on engagement and long-term retention, to a community model based on ongoing recovery and change with recovery contagion at its heart.

Key learning points

■ It is possible to attempt to quantify aspects of recovery capital, and the chapter presents data from a UK pilot study that has attempted to do this.

■ Quantifying recovery capital involves assessing basic 'enablers' of recovery defined as a safe place to live, some form of meaningful activity and abstinence from crack cocaine or opiate use. This is strongly linked to subjective well-being and quality of life. This overall model is associated with more positive treatment discharge reasons.

■ However, there are few existing measures that adequately quantify social capital and the chapter reviews local pilot site evidence for mapping supportive social networks.

References

Achara-Abrahams I, Evans A & King J (2011) Recovery-focused behavioural health system transformation: A framework for change and lessons learned from Philadelphia. In: J Kelly & W White (Eds) *Addiction Recovery Management: Theory, research and practice.* New York: Humana Springer: New York.

Best D & Laudet A (2010) *The Potential for Recovery Capital.* London: RSA.

Granfield R & Cloud W (2001) Social context and natural recovery: The role of social capital in the resolution of drug-related problems. *Substance Use and Misuse* 36 1543–1570.

Groshkova T, Best D & White W (2011) Recovery Group Participation Scale (RGPS): factor structure in alcohol and heroin recovery populations. *Journal of Groups in Addiction and Recovery* 6 76–92.

Groshkova T, Best D & White W (submitted) *The Assessment of Recovery Capital: Psychometric properties.*

Hibbert L & Best D (2011) Assessing recovery and functioning in former problem drinkers at different stages of their recovery journeys. *Drug and Alcohol Review* 30 12–20.

Marsden J, Farrell M, Bradbury C, Dale-Perera A, Eastwood B, Roxburgh M & Taylor S (2008) Development of the treatment outcomes profile. *Addiction* 103 (9) 1450–1460.

Moos (2011) Processes that promote recovery from addictive disorders. In J Kelly & & W White (Eds) *Addiction Recovery Management: Theory, research and practice.* New York: Humana Press, Springer.

Rethink (2008) *Getting Back to the World. Internal report.* London: Rethink.

Royal Society for the Arts (2010) *Connected Communities.* London: Royal Society for the Arts.

Wirral Drug Action Team (2009) *Annual Report.* Wirral: Wirral Drug Action Team.

Wirral Drug Action Team (2011) *The Road to Recovery.* Available at: http://www.wirraldaat.org/drugs/treatment/roadtorecovery.html (accessed October 2011).

Chapter 11

What works in recovery in the UK?

This chapter attempts to address three questions, with the main emphasis on the first.

1. What enables people to initiate recovery journeys and maintain them?
2. What can treatment services do to support and enable recovery progress?
3. What do we know about treatment systems that can support and develop recovery communities and hubs that promote recovery at the individual and family level?

The chapter will draw primarily on a growing and emerging UK evidence base about recovery but will also draw on knowledge from international research and evaluation work. This will pave the way for the final chapter, which overviews where the UK is in terms of the emerging recovery agenda, considers what the most important questions are that need to be addressed, and discusses what the future is likely to hold for the recovery movement.

Personal recovery journeys

There are a number of core areas in recovery journeys that have an emerging evidence base, notably recovery capital; developmental models of change; social networks and recovery; engaging with mutual aid groups and giving something back. Each area will be considered in turn and should be afforded equal prominence.

Recovery capital

Although there is a strong and evolving literature on social capital (Putnam, 2000; RSA, 2010a), it is really with the body of work around 'natural recovery' (Granfield & Cloud, 2001) that the concept of recovery capital was translated into the addiction field. This is based on the notion that there are resources (both personal and social) that an individual can draw upon to address their needs. White and Cloud (2008) argue that it is such positive resources (rather than levels of illness, pathology or complexity) that better predict the likelihood of long-term and sustainable recovery. Although Cloud and Granfield (2009) subsequently suggested that there may be a reverse currency ('negative recovery capital') that can reduce the likelihood of long-term positive change (caused by, for instance, severe mental health problems or a long history of imprisonment), the notion of recovery capital affords us two things. First, a strengths-based model for mapping ongoing positive growth in recovery and second, a potential metric for assessing and measuring the level of capital an individual possesses.

The additional suggestion that recovery capital may incorporate a third component – 'collective recovery capital' (Best & Laudet, 2010; RSA, 2010b) – provides a mechanism for assessing not only the resources an individual can call upon but the likely impact of their community and context on their recovery journey. In this model key aspects of the 'recovery environment' can be incorporated within the assessment of recovery sustainability. This will include:

- aspects of the provision of formal addictions treatment – in terms of access, evidence-based practice and crucially, in terms of the quality of staff and the capacity for meaningful therapeutic relationships

- the accessibility of recovery communities and recovery champions as discussed below

- the overall level of deprivation and the effect this has on the possibility of achieving a safe and sober living environment, of accessing training and employment and a high quality of life in a cohesive community.

The key point about recovery capital is that the three elements – personal, social and collective – are dynamically linked and that each ebbs and flows in relation to the others. If we are to develop a science of recovery, the unit of measurement will be recovery capital, and our ability to predict recovery stability will not attempt to guess what will happen to people (in terms of jobs, families, relationships or opportunities), but will look at the gradual accrual of resources, supports and strengths that will enable people to overcome life challenges. There is a separate challenge around the three parts of recovery capital, which is about weightings of specific resources and factors. The evidence would suggest that it is social networks that create the environment and context in which personal resources can flourish or diminish, but the evidence base around this remains limited.

One of the attempts at quantifying recovery capital has been the development of the Assessment of Recovery Capital (ARC) (Groshkova *et al*, in preparation). The original version contained 10 dimensions, each containing five items that were positive and five that were negative recovery indicators. However, field testing suggested that the scale was too long and that the negative items duplicated some acute assessment areas, and so it was amended to measure recovery strengths only, assessing five areas of personal recovery capital and five areas of social recovery capital. The key domains are set out in Table 11.1. Each item (of a total of 50) is endorsed if the individual completing the scale agrees and is left blank if they do not, providing a total score out of 25 for each of the domains – personal and social recovery capital with higher scores reflecting greater levels of capital. Psychometric testing suggests that the scale has good test-retest reliability and good concurrent validation when measured against the WHO Quality of Life scale (WHO, 2004).

Table 11.1: Domains of the assessment of recovery capital

Personal recovery capital	Social recovery capital
Physical health	Citizenship and community involvement
Psychological health	Social support
Substance use and sobriety	Meaningful activities
Coping and life functioning	Recovery experience
Housing and safety	Risk taking

The ARC scale provides a positive indicator of personal and social resource and it has been used in treatment effectiveness and recovery studies in the UK. As shown in Chapter 10, it correlates positively with the subjective well-being measures from the Treatment Outcomes Profile (TOP) (Marsden *et al,* 2008), and it offers clinicians a method for assessing positive changes in functioning and well-being that are positively valenced and that can direct clinical activities and motivate and engage clients in the recovery process. However, this work is at an early stage and there is still a considerable volume of research required to test the predictive utility of measurement of individual capital.

Developmental sequences

Furthermore, within a developmental model, it is anticipated that positive recovery capital is a necessary but not a sufficient factor in predicting long-term positive change for two reasons. Within the Best and Laudet (2010) and RSA (2010a) models, the scales omit one of the three dimensions (collective recovery capital) and do not account for developmental process. Each of these factors is critical in ensuring that recovery journeys are not over-predicted, which will always be predicated on context factors and unpredictable life events.

Contextual factors: The three areas of environmental influence are around specialist treatment, access to recovery hubs and communities and locality factors relating to opportunity, and access to recovery resources. While there is a considerable literature discussing processes of 'natural recovery' (Granfield & Cloud, 2001; Klingemann, 1991), treatment services have a pivotal role in recovery for many people, particularly those with the most entrenched problems. As White (2007) has discussed, one of the key aspects of treatment is ready access and effective engagement, but from a developmental perspective there is a particular issue around both engagement with specialist services and with counsellors or key workers. It is possible that treatment can constitute a 'turning point' in the addiction and recovery journey if it has sufficient salience and impact on the person. Thus, it is relatively easy to understand why residential rehabilitation, if it involves months spent in a new physical environment with a different set of social relations engaged in structured activities, is a significant life event. For community treatments – where the client remains in the same residence, attends the service often less than once a week, and is not obliged to change their daily routines – it is much harder to see a salient turning point. This is why Simpson's Treatment Process Model (2004) offers such an important construction of treatment and the therapeutic relationship. It is the therapeutic relationship embedded within an evidence-based model of delivering psychosocial interventions that is important.

To maintain the social influence model presented throughout this book, the key component of any possible turning point is interpersonal and rests with the worker's ability to generate and shape the motivation to change, the belief that recovery is possible and the establishment of social networks and personal resources that are needed. Thus, the key role for treatment services is about effective engagement, motivation-building and then partnership working in establishing the links to recovery champions and groups, and in

Addiction Recovery: A movement for social change and personal growth in the UK ©
Pavilion Publishing (Brighton) Ltd 2012

working to build the psychological and social resources that are needed. As a result of the length of time to stable recovery, it also involves a continuity of care and support beyond any acute episodes of treatment and the provision of early re-engagement activities for any lapses that may occur.

Specialist and more generic treatments will also be necessary for the effective management of acute symptoms and ongoing chronic problems, but is unlikely to be sufficient without adequate peer-based support systems. This is the second aspect of 'collective' recovery capital that can be measured and assessed. While there is a considerable literature showing the benefits of 12-step mutual aid groups (Humphrey, 2004; White, 2009), there are other recovery options that may indicate the maturity of a recovery system. This relates to the diversity of groups and champions, and the visibility and accessibility of community recovery supports.

White (2007) has spoken of the importance of peer-based recovery support services, but the evidence from the UK would suggest that the accessibility and visibility of these groups is critical, and that they need to offer a diverse range of options. Best (2010) has argued that the recovery groups need to provide access to mainstreaming activities (education and training support as well as engagement in a range of community activities), in leisure and interest activities (fishing clubs, football teams, walking and arts groups) as well as recovery-focused community activities such as mutual aid groups and peer-led aftercare support. What makes such groups a positive component of the recovery environment is their attractiveness and their ability to engage and support people in and out of treatment. Finally, there are broader contextual issues relating to the socio-economic context, in particular:

- access to sober living housing

- access to opportunities for education and training, as well as volunteering and job opportunities

- the wider cohesion of the community, including its level of prejudice and stigma in relation to addiction and its awareness of the recovery agenda.

This wider context provides the basis for a measurement of the 'recovery friendliness' of the environment and the extent to which opportunities for change will arise and what the contextual supports will be for sustaining them.

Life events and trajectories: The basic developmental model presented here is that individuals will experience potential windows of opportunity for change both as a result of single events and the impact of accumulation of discrete experiences. The impact of these 'windows' of opportunity for change will depend on the three components of recovery capital:

1. personal capital

2. social capital

3. contextual capital.

Thus, for a successful transition, the individual will need certain positive personal qualities and skills – these may well include motivation, determination, hope, and basic life and coping skills. These raw ingredients will need to be fostered in social contexts and settings that are supportive and positive and that provide both support and modelling for ongoing recovery. And finally, this core will need to be embedded within a wider community context that enables the growth of personal and social capital, providing access to recovery models and the 'mainstreaming' options needed to give the person a safe place to live and the opportunities for engaging in a range of vocational and leisure activities that are a prerequisite of both quality of life and stable recovery.

The role that recovery capital plays is twofold – the first is that it is a safety net. For individuals who have strong personal and social capital, the threat to ongoing recovery is less where there is a strong set of personal skills and these are embedded within a positive social network that supports recovery. So where there is positive capital, all candidate turning points are more likely to have positive outcomes and conclusions. But there is a second type of impact that positive recovery capital will have – it will increase the likelihood that positive events will happen and that key life events will be experienced as part of a positive recovery trajectory. While there are some life events that an individual will have little control over – for example, the death of parents, relationship break-ups and physical ill-health – there are others that will occur partly because of the resources an individual has and the networks they mix in. Thus, for people who have developed a positive personal identity, good self-esteem and a sense of self-efficacy, opportunities that arise (for instance, for a new job or a new relationship) are more likely to be grasped. Likewise, people who have a dynamic and large social network are more likely to come into contact with opportunities for personal development. One of the key conclusions from social network research is that it is friends of friends who are likely to be the key contacts in accessing community resources – such as knowledge about services, opportunities for training courses or jobs, or social events in the local neighbourhood (Putnam, 2000; RSA, 2010a). Thus, the tripartite model of recovery capital (personal, social and collective) is both about the quality of the painter and also about the canvas – in combination, they will influence not only the ability to grasp opportunities but also the probability that the opportunities will arise in the first place.

Influencing the collective field

Not everyone who recovers will need to access specialist services, nor will they all need to engage with recovery or mutual aid groups in the community. So the idea of developing systems to enable recovery is not based on the notion that all individuals will benefit. The history of natural recovery would suggest that there are some individuals who will pass through addiction problems but will resolve these within their own social networks and support systems. However, for many people that will not be the case and the remaining section of this chapter is about what wider society can do to enable lasting recovery.

Treatment

The immediate aim of treatment does not change in a recovery model – to offer immediate and equable access to problem substance users, to assess and intervene to address acute physical and psychological health, and to offer medications and therapeutic interventions as required. It is important to reiterate at this point that there is nothing incompatible about harm reduction and recovery models – for many individuals in the early stages of their recovery journeys, there will be little difference between the detached work of harm reduction and the assertive community activities promoted in recovery models (eg. White, 2007; Valentine, 2011). At least as far as the author is concerned, there is also no incompatibility between needle exchanges or the provision of naloxone to prevent overdose fatality and the recovery agenda, which is a long-term and developmental process that will require phased interventions to match both the stage of readiness and the immediate needs. Acute needs will continue to predominate in the development of intervention plans.

However, that does not mean that recovery implies 'business as usual' for specialist treatment providers, and there are fundamental shifts in both philosophy and practice that are necessitated by a shift to a recovery model, as have been articulated in the recovery-oriented systems work reported in Chapter 8 (Achara-Abrahams *et al,* 2011; Kirk, 2011; Valentine, 2011). Within a UK perspective, this involves a dramatic shift in processes and practices away from a 'specialist centre' model where individuals are 'treated' to a community-based partnership model where most of the key recovery activities will take place outside the specialist centres and there is a much less clear assumption that the clinician is the expert who holds the answers and possibly the cure. It is also a shift away from a model based on pessimistic assumptions of change to a fundamental belief that recovery is possible and realistic for most clients.

In this model there are changes that are necessary at both the client–therapist level and in systems and structures within organisations. At the therapeutic level, the first shift is from a 'pathology' to a strengths model with the assumption that the process is led by the client and that the aim of treatment is effective engagement with recovery groups and communities and is likely to be based on active engagement in meaningful activities. For this, the worker not only needs to understand the principles of recovery, they also need to know the community in which they work. Only by having this knowledge are workers able to link people into the community resources and supports they will need, and be able to introduce their clients to recovery champions and recovery hubs that will meet their needs.

Within the recovery model, there is also increased emphasis on the therapeutic alliance as a potential developmental turning point. The biggest challenge to all workers, mentors and peers within a recovery model is the ability to inspire hope and belief in their clients and to create a shared set of goals and aims that are based on trust and commitment to common goals and values. This is an enormous task – and is virtually impossible when workers have caseloads that can be in excess of 50, as is common in the UK. What we are asking here is that the worker can represent a beacon of hope, a mentor, an inspiration and a guide to their clients. This does not mean that the workers have to be in recovery themselves, but it does mean that they have to be more than case (or prescription) managers. Yet it does happen – in many recovery stories in the UK, individual workers are named as having had that transformative effect and it is no less than this that we would want from recovery workers.

For this to be possible, the service has to have an interface and infrastructure that enables and supports change. It is asking a lot of workers to inspire and motivate, guide and support people with complex and entrenched problems, but it is simply not possible if the worker has large caseloads and operates in a service where the primary aim is to retain large numbers of clients in long-term prescribing treatments, with little wraparound or psychosocial interventions. Fixed weekly, fortnightly or monthly slots of between 20–60 minutes are only consistent with a managerialist model of treatment, particularly if these time limits are set by the worker and do not empower or enable the client to own the sessions.

Thus, managers have to be creative and imaginative in establishing a working ethos that supports and enables their workers to develop meaningful, trusting and therapeutic relationships that are not restricted to brief sessions of case management and the supervision of medication. This may necessitate some kind of segmentation of the caseload so that clients who are engaged and motivated are provided with the intensity of support they need. This means two things: first, flexibility and motivation in individual workers to identify, promote and enable recovery progress and activity in clients, and second, effective opportunities for bridging.

This is something that some services already do, but is not accorded the importance or priority it deserves. It is critical that each team conducts some form of Asset Based Community Development (Kretzmann & McKnight, 1993) – an assertive audit and review of the resources and supports available in their local area, and that these audits produce networks of key individuals, rather than simply producing a list of local agencies. Each worker needs to know about the professional and community services that are available in their locale and have sufficient active engagement with these groups and agencies that there are individual names and contact numbers available to the team. Each member of staff should be encouraged to visit the services and develop working relationships with both peers and professionals so that they are able to pick up a phone and make direct contact on behalf of their clients.

This is part of a culture change model in which specialist services are seen not as expert deliverers of rigid interventions but as a component in a community system of delivering ongoing support and care that is holistic and culturally embedded. The notion of 'silos' of care where specialist services, community-based groups and community and mutual aid organisations operate in the same areas but with little engagement and overlap is not compatible with a recovery model based on continuity of care, empowerment and choice. A recovery service must recognise that it does not have the science or the resource to attempt to provide all of the answers, and so recognise and embrace different philosophies and models that will be linked to individual needs at different points in the recovery journey.

The underlying model that service managers and staff must aspire to is openness and permeability. This means that clients and workers should aim to provide interventions both inside and outside of 'physical centres', and that where such specialist centres exist, they should be regarded as community assets and recovery hubs. In other words, specialist treatment settings should welcome and embrace visits and activities undertaken by community groups and, where resources and time permit, specialist workers should engage in community activities outside of their specialist hubs. The unit of effectiveness is the recovery community, not the specialist treatment provider. This applies especially to making recovery champions – attractive and visible icons of recovery success – visible to people at earlier stages of their recovery journeys. The point of this is to provide role models for recovery and to provide living evidence that recovery is possible. The recovery awareness of service managers and their own engagement with the recovery movement will have a significant effect on establishing a recovery-friendly culture in treatment services.

Systems and commissioning

While much of the excitement that has been generated in the UK has resulted from community-driven recovery groups and activities, the role of 'strategic leadership' should not be under-estimated. In several of the successful US models (Kirk, 2011; Achara-Abrahams *et al*, 2011), vision and leadership have played a critical role in the early establishment of a recovery philosophy and its successful implementation. Among the key issues identified are the clear establishment and dissemination of a recovery model – described generally as a vision that creates a set of goals and principles that can be derived from the existing literature, and that is consistent with principles of empowerment and choice, self-determination, ongoing support and continuity of care and the transition to a predominantly peer-based approach.

The creation of such a model will require clarity and commitment from a coalition of sector leaders that, in a UK context, will require the support and active engagement of the commissioners of specialist treatment services. The evidence (as outlined in Kelly and White's (2011) *Addiction Recovery Management: Theory, research and practice*) would suggest that the 'early adopters' of such a model must create a coalition of support that will enable the translation of a high-level vision into a plan for implementation that has the engagement and commitment of a range of stakeholders. It is crucial that the more successful elements of the existing treatment system – governance and high standards of clinical care – are not lost, but this is an approach that is more revolution than evolution and will involve ongoing monitoring and mapping of four core domains.

1. Organisational commitment and engagement across the specialist service and into linked services such as mental health providers, criminal justice agencies, housing providers and education and training services.

2. Changes in the daily practices and procedures in clinical practice including assessment and review processes, the use of medications and the active engagement of service users and recovery community groups in the delivery of specialist services. At its heart, the 'diagnostic' for the success of this transition is the change in culture among professional staff – their attitudes and beliefs about recovery and their engagement in the ongoing recovery journeys of their clients.

3. The growth and development of a diverse range of recovery services and communities that take an increasingly central role in supporting alcohol and drug addicts prior to their engagement with specialist services, while such treatments are ongoing and after formal treatment is complete.

4. Such a large agenda, and such a radical change in processes and roles, will not be achieved overnight and the evidence would suggest that such a transformation will take around 5–10 years to achieve. For this reason, it is important to create a plan that will allow monitoring over long periods of time. Kotter (1996) suggests that, with such a long-term programme, it is critical that some 'quick wins' are identified and communicated effectively to a wide range of stakeholders.

In a UK context, this will involve fundamental shifts in the performance management process and a transition to outcome monitoring that is focused on sustainable recovery journeys and the community resources that will be necessary to enable and deliver this. A range of indicators that can include people in recovery, family members, staff attitudes, service activities and community groups should be considered and tailored to local needs. This will be radically different to the recent process measures that have dominated in England for drug services in particular.

Internationally, it is still an early stage in the development of monitoring and performance management measures for the recovery movement but these should include both subjective and experiential measures for individuals' experiences of the recovery journey and the quality of treatment services delivered, as well as more objective indicators that will include size and number of visible recovery communities and effective 'bridging' between the treatment and recovery services. There is also no reason why recovery models should not be subjected to the same rigorous assessments of cost effectiveness, as has been demonstrated by Boyle *et al* (2011). It is critical for the credibility and evolution of the recovery movement that it is subjected to the same levels of academic rigour that exist for other forms of service delivery.

The final core role for the strategic development of a recovery model is around the implementation of Asset Based Community Development (ABCD) (Kretzmann & McKnight, 1993). Kretzmann and McKnight (1993) argue that *'Communities have never been built upon their deficiencies. Building communities has always depended on mobilising the capacity and assets of people and place'*. This agenda is about identifying and mobilising resources in the community that can enable and sustain recovery activity and can be used as a part of the process of kick-starting the coalitions and community integration that is central to a recovery model. This is partly a model for mainstreaming with wider community development issues and is also about addressing and challenging stigma in the community.

In a UK context, Marmot *et al* argue that *'When practitioners begin with a focus on what communities have (their assets) as opposed to what they don't have (their needs) a community's efficacy in addressing its own needs increases, as does its capacity to lever in external support. It provides healthy community practitioners with a fresh perspective on building bridges with socially excluded people and marginalised groups'* (Marmot *et al*, 2010, p3). This involves engaging and inspiring the key local resources – workers who are willing to go that 'extra mile', people in recovery and other key figures in the local community in kick-starting a process of social engagement. The rationale for this is that the idea of contagion applies as much to professionals as it does to people starting their own recovery journeys.

Across England there are early attempts at generating recovery communities that are based on the idea of asset mapping and development – that bringing 'early adopters' together to create an inventory of the key resources and supports for recovery is both an act of engagement and motivation as well as an early step in establishing a list of resources and physical assets that can be tapped into. For instance, our early work with 'recovery champion' professionals in Bradford (Yorkshire) generated the following ideas:

- a recovery logo

- a recovery website

- a recovery walk

- a recovery wall based on stories of recovery

- a recovery communications strategy.

Some of these ideas are being taken forward and others will fall by the wayside, but what has happened through this activity is the emergence of a self-selected group of addiction professionals who are working together – often in their own time – to identify, link and augment existing resources under the flag of a recovery community. The role for the commissioners is both as participant and enabler – to make sure that they can mobilise management resources in the specialist addiction area and other key link services such as mental health and housing, and to provide strategic direction and resource to inspire and promote the quick wins.

Precisely the same mechanisms of attraction – a sense of belief that recovery is possible, an identification with the group and a clear sense of purpose – will work for professionals in the same way that it works for people in recovery, and will generate that 'hub' of enthusiasm and motivation that will attract others to engage in the process. And this is the final key role for the strategic leader – to ensure that these levels of innovation and action are adequately linked and supported. The emerging UK recovery community model is predicated on activities at the community, therapeutic and strategic levels but these activities require strategic co-ordination and linkage. However, it is the work of the recovery groups that will offer the possibility of 'quick wins' that can be communicated and disseminated to provide momentum and to challenge the scepticism of those who do not commit to the early stages of the recovery movement.

Conclusion

The emergence of a recovery movement in the UK has been based largely on the activities of a diverse range of recovery communities and groups. However, the publication of recovery strategies in both Scotland and England has offered a mechanism for mainstreaming this work by engaging professionals and strategic leaders in local communities. There is a risk with this model that the indigenous recovery communities could be professionalised and brought within specialist services that may minimise or neuter their impact, and so it is imperative that peer ownership is central to the evolution of this model. It is still too early to assess the impact of recovery communities but the diverse array of local initiatives and emerging coalitions of recovery would suggest that there are considerable grounds for optimism about the longevity of a recovery movement in the UK. The final chapter returns to the question 'Where is the recovery community and its underlying evidence base?' and looks to the future to speculate what will be needed to ensure the success of the recovery endeavour as the heartbeat of a systemic response to addiction.

Key learning points

■ There is a growing and supportive evidence base about 'what works' in recovery in the UK.

■ There is a common method for measuring the 'quantity' of recovery resources available at both a personal and a community level.

■ There are key aspects of specialised treatment including accessibility and delivery of evidence-based interventions, and about specialist workers, relating to their ability to inspire belief and to link individuals early in recovery journeys to groups and communities.

■ There is also a need to prioritise transformation in specialist services to commit more to activities in communities and to link to groups who can support and enable personal change.

■ This transformation also requires system leadership and the ability to inspire and motivate services to change to promote recovery activities and values.

References

Achara-Abrahams I, Evans A & King J (2011) Recovery-focused behavioural health system transformation: A framework for change and lessons learned from Philadelphia. In: J Kelly & W White (Eds) *Addiction Recovery Management: Theory, research and practice.* New York: Humana Springer.

Best D & Laudet A (2010) *The Potential for Recovery Capital.* London: RSA.

Best D (2010) *Recovery Manual for Worcestershire.* Unpublished report.

Boyle M, Loveland D & George S (2011) Implementing recovery management in a treatment system. In: J Kelly & W White (Eds) *Addiction Recovery Management: Theory, research and practice.* New York: Humana Springer.

Cloud W & Granfield R (2009) Conceptualising recovery capital: expansion of a theoretical construct. *Substance Use and Misuse* **42** (12/13) 1971–1986.

Granfield R & Cloud W (2001) Social context and natural recovery: The role of social capital in the resolution of drug-related problems. *Substance Use and Misuse* **36** 1543–1570.

Groshkova T, Best D & White W (in preparation) *The Assessment of Recovery Capital: Psychometric properties.*

Humphrey K (2004) *Circles of Recovery: Self-help organisations for addictions.* Cambridge: Cambridge University Press.

Kelly J & White W (2001) *Addiction Recovery Management: Theory, research and practice.* New York: Springer Science.

Kirk T (2011) Connecticut's journey to a state-wide recovery-oriented health-care system: Strategies, successes and challenges. In: J Kelly & W White (Eds) *Addiction Recovery Management: Theory, research and practice.* New York: Humana Springer.

Klingemann H (1991) The motivation for change from problem alcohol and heroin use. *British Journal of Addiction* **86** 727–744.

Kotter J (1996) *Leading Change.* Massachusetts: Harvard Business School Press.

Kretzmann J & McKnight J (1993) *Building Communities from the Inside Out: A path towards finding and mobilising a community's assets.* Evanston, IL: ABCD Institute.

Marmot Review (2010) *Fair Society, Healthy Lives: Strategic Review of Health Inequalities in England post-2010.* Available at: http://www.marmotreview.org/AssetLibrary/pdfs/Reports/FairSocietyHealthyLives.pdf (accessed October 2011).

Marsden J, Farrell M, Bradbury C, Dale-Perera A, Eastwood, B, Roxburgh M & Taylor S (2008) Development of the Treatment Outcomes Profile. *Addiction* **103** (9) 1450–1460.

Putnam R (2000) *Bowling Alone: The collapse and revival of the American community.* New York: Simon and Schuster.

Royal Society for the Arts (2010a) *Whole Person Recovery: A user-centred systems approach to alcohol and drug services.* London: Royal Society for the Arts.

Royal Society for the Arts (2010b) *Connected Communities.* London: Royal Society for the Arts.

Simpson DD (2004) A conceptual framework for drug treatment processes and outcomes. *Journal of Substance Abuse Treatment* **27** (2) 99–121.

Valentine P (2011) Peer based recovery support services within a recovery community organisation: The CCAR experience. In: J Kelly & W White (Eds) *Addiction Recovery Management: Theory, research and practice.* London: Humana Springer.

White W (2007) A recovery revolution in Philadelphia. *Counselor* **8** (5) 34–38.

White W & Cloud W (2008) Recovery capital: A primer for addiction professionals. *Counselor* **9** (5) 22–27.

White W (2009) The mobilisation of community resources to support long-term addiction recovery. *Journal of Substance Abuse Treatment* **36** (2) 146–158.

World Health Organisation (2004) The World Health Organisation Quality of Life -BREF (WHOQOL-BREF). Available at: http://www.who.int/substance_abuse/research_tools/whoqolbref/en (accessed October 2011).

Chapter 12

What now?

This chapter provides an honest and personal overview of the recovery movement in the UK. It attempts to rebut some of the criticisms of the approach and reviews the strengths and weaknesses of its achievements. A personal view of what the future may hold then follows, with a particular focus on what the gaps are at present and how these might be addressed. The primary purpose of this chapter is to provoke discussion and debate about the need for a strategic direction and leadership for the recovery movement, and the risks associated with relying on a disparate collection of ground-up community-based initiatives.

Is there a recovery movement, and what does it look like?

One of the criticisms often advanced against the notion of a movement is that *'this is nothing new'* (Best *et al,* 2010). In one sense this is self-evident; people have been recovering from alcohol, illicit drugs and other addictive behaviours for longer than there has been something called 'recovery'. It is also fair to say that many of the principles of recovery thinking are not new, such as personal empowerment, engagement of and in families and communities, self-determination and staged and phased interventions. However, the notion of strategic co-ordination and the 'co-production' of visible communities of recovery as the leading and central focus of addiction response is a new approach, as is the systematic attempt to develop an evidence base to both quantify the numbers of people in recovery and to map out the most common roads to recovery (RSA, 2010).

These two endeavours are not independent. To actively engage policymakers and professional groups, it is important that a credible research and practice evidence base emerges. There are two 'truths' that have currency in the recovery community that are problematic:

■ recovery is an impenetrably personal experience

■ people will 'find' recovery only when they are ready.

These are compounded by practical issues of sampling – many who are in recovery are not accessible because their lives have moved on, because they are members of anonymous fellowships or because their recovery involved a 'natural recovery' process. Therefore, researchers engaging in this area need to be more creative, imaginative and dynamic in developing designs and methods than the clinical equivalents. There is also extremely limited research funding currently available across the addictions field and particularly for questions relating to recovery. Yet the rewards of recovery research more than compensate for this. Recovery stories are narratives of hope, re-birth, purpose and growth, embedded within a sense of gratitude and social sensitivity, and researching those at every stage of this process is impossible without being 'infected' by aspects of recovery's positive qualities.

A further problem stems from funding limitations. As yet, much of the recovery rhetoric in both the English and Scottish drug strategies remains untested empirically, providing a foundation for resistance and scepticism. It is also difficult to attract professional researchers and academics to an area where there is limited opportunity for research funding, which in turn creates a vicious circle. The situation in the UK currently is that there is a limited evidence base, prompting some resistance and reluctance to engage with the recovery agenda by the research community, which in turn means that there continue to be gaps in knowledge, prompting further concerns that recovery is an area of work that sits outside an evidenced framework.

Yet, the situation is beginning to change as not only is there an emerging UK evidence base, there is also increasing linkage and co-ordination of research activity between British and North American researchers, and the increasing emergence of evaluation data around recovery services and programmes. Indeed, the Glasgow Recovery Study also relied on the support and engagement of AA groups and members to recruit participants (Best *et al,* 2011). There is also an increasing level of engagement and support from recovery groups for research, along with the recognition that supporting evidence will be essential to the growth of the UK recovery movement. The links to the evaluation process and to increased visibility has also assisted in raising the profile and communication of the recovery movement.

The sense of hope and contagion does not apply only at local level. The existence of the online community Wired In, the success of the two UK recovery walks and the ongoing prominence and visibility of the North-West Recovery Forum have provided a set of recovery hubs at a national level that have allowed alliances and activities across areas to coalesce and enabled the emergence of a learning culture and a supportive environment for local activities. The strength of a recovery movement will always be based on grassroots activity, but the development of national activities and forums has enabled a more mature debate and a broader perspective to develop.

What are the strengths and weaknesses of the UK recovery movement at present?

Probably the biggest strength of the movement to date has been the emergence of innovation, creativity and success over adversity as common principles that have united a diverse set of activities, groups and personalities. The success in generating raised political consciousness has formalised a systemic response (at least in England) and has engaged and 'infected' a much wider group of decision makers and brought them into contact with a population that may previously have been 'hidden'. This combination of emerging energy in a range of local communities supplemented by national political drivers has generated movement in a treatment system that had become, in some areas at least, moribund and 'stuck'.

This increased scrutiny of recovery groups and communities has afforded a major opportunity for raising awareness that recovery happens, spreads through social networks, and is embedded in communities and groups. This has created a space for re-invigorating the specialist workforce and increasing the likelihood that individuals previously unaware of recovery and its embodiments will be exposed to the contagion of recovery. As with the key facets of individual change, so the underlying principles of collective recovery adhere to the same principles and processes.

A sense of hope: The growth of a range of recovery representation groups across the UK – although leading to competing and discordant voices and interpersonal squabbling – is indicative of a sense of movement and dynamism that continues to grow, driven by a social contagion of recovery and the recognition of a shared and powerful voice for change and self-determination. At heart the movement for recovery is a movement of hope, challenging the professional mantra of a 'chronic, relapsing condition' and replacing professional compromises with a collective aspirational belief that 'I can't but we can'.

A sense of purpose: The added value of the recovery model is personal growth embedded within and inextricably linked to the emergence of a movement with a set of aspirations and values as laid out in the CSAT (2009) guidelines. In the UK, these have emerged particularly as the need for a 'voice', empowerment and self-determination and the belief that recovery is about changing in the community and changes of those communities. Although there is a diverse array of philosophies and approaches to recovery, most have a component of 'giving back' as the binding mechanism towards shared hope and purpose.

A sense of belonging: Although the evidence base is still at an early stage, the evidence is very clear about the intrinsic social quality of recovery. Where Moos (2011) speaks of social control and social learning as underlying principles, this translates as a sense of individual growth embedded within a sense of belonging. Identification with mutual aid groups, therapeutic communities and recovery forums is about that emerging sense of purpose vivified though social action.

Where now for the UK recovery movement?

The sections below cover three main areas – strategic development, local activities and the evolution of recovery services embedded within recovery systems, and the key questions of research and science.

Strategy and the future

As Best and Ball (2011) argue, there is currently a translation problem. There are extremely positive policies around recovery, but there are problems in translating this policy into practice, particularly as the policies are accompanied by a switch to a commitment to de-centralised control of implementation. This is in part a problem of articulating a language of recovery – how do we measure something so personal, and how do we know when it has been achieved? The sophistication of thinking is growing at a much faster rate among policy makers and practitioners in England than in Scotland, with segmentation and the introduction of Payment by Results formalising mechanisms for shaping recovery targets and developing a language to map and measure recovery activities and progress. However, this is a complex and ongoing process that will require sufficient flexibility that individual and personal experiences are accounted for and that community impact and socially embedded objectives – such as the impact of recovery on families and wider communities – are also assessed. There is also a real challenge around the relationship between recovery goals and treatment goals, with some justification for treating these as separate domains of the same endeavour.

Recovery services and systems

At the moment there is a wonderful diversity of community and recovery groups emerging through individual skills and motivation and local needs at various levels of linkage and co-ordination with formal treatment providers. The emergence of models of effective linkage between recovery support programmes and mainstream treatment providers has yet to be articulated clearly in a UK context. There are some big challenges that face the emergence of meaningful recovery services and some key questions need to be answered.

■ Is there such a thing as medically-assisted recovery in the UK? If so, how prevalent is it, and would it still exist if adequate abstinent recovery options were available?

■ If recovery success can happen in the context of opiate substitution prescribing, how can recovery communities be supported and emerge in the context of methadone and buprenorphine prescribing?

■ How can specialist services be convinced that community recovery groups have a meaningful role to play, and to actively engage in partnership work with community groups? This challenge applies particularly to addiction psychiatry and to specialist GPs in the UK, who have been sceptical and slow to accept the merits of a recovery approach.

■ How do commissioners build the support from partnerships for the recovery strategy and plans over long periods of time and generate locally meaningful measures of recovery that are convincing and linked to models of cost effectiveness?

What do we need to know about recovery?

In attempting to lay out a programme of suggested research work for the UK, we could do worse than look at the incredible programmatic work undertaken in the US, particularly by William White and Alexandre Laudet. However, in broad themes, some of the key questions follow.

Prevalence and incidence

How big are the recovery populations across the UK? And what is the size of the 'visible' recovery population? Within this question are variations by patterns of substance use (including but not restricted to questions of alcohol and heroin recovery), by age and gender profile, by geographic region, and in terms of the clustering of recovery groups and communities, and formal treatment services. CSAT's (2009) estimate that 58% of all those who develop a substance dependence will eventually achieve stable recovery is a statistic that needs to be tested in a UK context, with some confidence intervals and conditions established around that figure.

Individual recovery triggers

What are the catalysts that enable people to start recovery journeys? We know from research in the UK (Best *et al*, 2008; Best *et al*, 2011) that people often speak of 'maturing out' but it would also be important to know what social and intervention factors support the initial decision to start a recovery journey and allow it to become a reality.

Individual recovery sustaining factors

White and Kurtz (2006) estimate that it takes between five and seven years for opiate users to enter 'stable recovery' from the point of abstinence. This provokes questions of applicability in a UK context, questions around what causes variability in the time taken for this process and how it is possible to recognise what this means. This links to ongoing questions of definition and operationalisation (as discussed in Chapter 1) and may require refinement in terms of differing criteria or components at each stage of the recovery journey.

Recovery and who can help

Much of the discussion in this book has focused on the intrinsically social processes underlying recovery, yet our understanding of this process – and indeed our instruments for measuring interpersonal engagement and interpersonal capital – remain limited. These issues will involve both positive and negative social factors, including the impact of using peers and family members, as well as the importance of role models in enabling transitions to meaningful recovery.

Addiction Recovery: A movement for social change and personal growth in the UK ©
Pavilion Publishing (Brighton) Ltd 2012

Recovery and what works

In the UK, where there is a strong commitment in policy to a recovery approach, it is essential that workers and services are supported to enable positive changes and to maximise the recovery outcomes their clients achieve. This will include the systems lessons discussed in Chapter 7 as well as the important issues of what treatment models and processes increase the effective transition to recovery groups and communities. In particular, there is a huge need – in the UK and internationally – for a better understanding of the types of aftercare that can be provided and how they enable transition to recovery communities, and also about the ongoing support services that people are likely to need.

While there is a substantial evidence base about treatment, there is much less known about the period of post-acute treatment and, if the White and Kurtz model of post-treatment recovery journeys is accurate, then there needs to be a stronger science of matching individuals with packages of care, about intensity of treatment options and about the effectiveness of different programmes and interventions. However, this will not just be about specialist addiction treatment – it will also be about housing and options for training, education and employment; about links to mutual aid groups and the emergence of community groups that are not mutual aid focused. Finally, this will also link to strategic direction questions of how to support the growth of recovery hubs and recovery communities.

For this to happen, adequate measurement techniques will be necessary that allow for the assessment of initiation of recovery processes and journeys – measures of individual recovery progress, of staff attitudes, cultures and practices, of community engagement and of the growth of recovery networks and their champions. These will need to take the form of both summary performance indicator measures as well as more substantial and robust tested instruments of recovery activity.

A final comment – is the UK an innovative centre of recovery?

In spite of some of the more gloomy conclusions reached above, the answer to this question overall is an unequivocal 'yes'. Across the UK, there is such a dramatic growth in diverse recovery activities that inspire individuals, families and communities that the term 'movement' is not an overstatement. Sustained in part by the new technologies of email, web and social networking sites, it is possible for that inspiration and interpersonal drive to be transmitted across geographical areas and for lessons to be learned in remote as well as urban locations. There is much work to be done but the UK is at the forefront of recovery inspiration and innovation, and it is now the task of the scientists, policymakers and particularly practitioners to attempt to catch up and make their contribution to a movement that will benefit from their involvement, but will not perish in their absence.

Key learning points

■ This is a new and emerging field that offers incredible opportunities to people from all kinds of backgrounds to participate in a social movement of hope.

■ The science is young and still developing a set of techniques and methods commensurate with the demands of a shifting paradigm of science.

■ This approach will be much more inclusive and the outcomes will be both personal and community-focused.

■ The recovery movement has provoked considerable resistance from some entrenched interest groups and this requires a focus on culture and organisational change.

■ However, ultimately, this is a message and a model of hope and the recovery movement will transcend petty and personal interests as it is a movement of social justice and emerging community development.

References

Best D & Ball G (2011) Recovery and public policy: driving the strategy by raising political awareness. *Journal of Groups in Addiction and Recovery* **6** 7–19.

Best D, Ghufran S, Day E, Ray R & Loaring J (2008) Breaking the habit: a retrospective analysis of desistance factors among formerly problematic heroin users. *Drug and Alcohol Review* **27** (6) 619–624.

Best D, Bamber S, Battersby A, Gilman M, Groshkova T, Honor S, McCartney D & Yates R (2010) Recovery and straw men: An analysis of the objections raised to the transition to a recovery model in UK addiction services. *Journal of Groups in Addiction and Recovery* **5** (3–4) 264–288.

Best D, Gow J, Knox A, Taylor A, Groshkova T & White W (2011) Mapping the recovery stories of drinkers and drug users in Glasgow: Quality of life and its associations with measures of recovery capital. *Drug and Alcohol Review* DOI 10.1111.

Centre for Substance Abuse Treatment (2009) *Guiding Principles and Elements of Recovery Orientated Systems of Care: What do we know from the research?* Rockville, MD: Substance Abuse and Mental Health Services Administration.

Moos (2011) Processes that promote recovery from addictive disorders. In: J Kelly & W White (Eds) *Addiction Recovery Management: Theory, research and practice.* New York: Humana Press, Springer.

Royal Society for the Arts (2010) *Connected Communities.* London: Royal Society for the Arts.

White W & Kurtz E (2006) The varieties of recovery experience. *International Journal of Self Help and Self Care* **3** (1–2) 21–61.